Contaminated land

Investigation, assessment and remediation

ICE design and practice guides

One of the major aims of the Institution of Civil Engineers is to provide its members with opportunities for continuing professional development. One method by which the Institution is achieving this is the production of design and practice guides on topics relevant to the professional activities of its members. The purpose of the guides is to provide an introduction to the main principles and important aspects of the particular subject, and to offer guidance as to appropriate sources for more detailed information. The guides aim to supplement and enhance existing authoritative and competent guidance documents prepared by key organisations such as central government, the Construction Industry Research and Information Association (CIRIA) and the Building Research Establishment (BRE).

The Institution has targeted as its principal audience practising civil engineers who are not expert in or familiar with the subject matter. This group includes recently graduated engineers who are undergoing their professional training and more experienced engineers whose work experience has not previously led them into the subject area in any detail. Those professionals who are more familiar with the subject may also find the guides of value as a handy overview or summary of the principal issues.

Where appropriate, the guides will feature checklists to be used as an *aide-mémoire* on major aspects of the subject and will provide, through references and bibliographies, guidance on authoritative, relevant and up-to-date published documents to which reference should be made for reliable and more detailed guidance.

ICE design and practice guide

Contaminated land

Investigation, assessment and remediation

Mary Harris and Sue Herbert

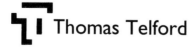 Thomas Telford

Published by Thomas Telford Services Ltd, Thomas Telford House, 1 Heron Quay, London, E14 4JD

First published 1994

A catalogue record for this book is available from the British Library

Classification:
Availability: Unrestricted
Content: Recommendations based on current practice
Status: Refereed
User: Practising civil engineers and designers

ISBN: 0 7277 2016 3

Typeset in Goudy Old Style 10.5/12 pt using Corel Ventura 4.2 at Thomas Telford Services Ltd.

Printed and Bound in Great Britain by The Lavenham Press, Sudbury, Suffolk.

Foreword

Contaminated land is a subject of increasing relevance and importance to civil engineers today as the need to reclaim and recycle land strengthens, associated with growing pressure on land resources and greater environmental awareness.

Contamination involves many issues, both technical and non-technical, and it is important that professionals working in this subject area appreciate at the outset the necessity of involving experts in several different disciplines. In addition to civil and geotechnical engineering, expertise will be required in chemistry, environmental science, geology, hydrogeology and project management, and may be needed in other subjects such as chemical or process engineering, ecology, biology, valuation and other financial matters and legislation. Practising civil or geotechnical engineers should not assume that their expertise will allow them to address all aspects of a contaminated land project adequately.

Contamination can affect the ground, water or air. This guide concentrates on land contamination, which includes the water environment. Contamination can occur through the presence of chemical substances, either in solid or liquid form, and from noxious and hazardous gases. Some reference is made to gas contamination, but the principal aim of the guide is to address chemical contamination of solids or liquids. Comprehensive guidance on gas contamination is currently being prepared by CIRIA, with a number of key documents recently published, and BRE have also produced valuable guidance on this subject. Certain aspects of land contamination are particularly specialised, such as radioactivity or some forms of military contamination such as explosives or chemical weapons. These subjects are not addressed in the guide and expert advice must always be sought in this respect.

Acknowledgements

This guide has been prepared by Dr Mary Harris of ECOTEC Research and Consulting (now with Clayton Environmental Consultants) under contract to the Institution of Civil Engineers. The contract was directed and managed by Mrs Sue Herbert of TBV Science, as the ICE Ground Board's Environment Champion.

The contributions and assistance of the following in reviewing the text are gratefully acknowledged:

Dr Robert Mair	Geotechnical Consulting Group (Ground Board Chairman)
Dr Bryan Gregory	Kirk McClure and Morton
Dr Andrew Lord	Ove Arup and Partners
Dr Terry Mellors	Independent Consultant
Mr Neil Trenter	Sir William Halcrow and Partners
Mr John Woodward	Independent Consultant

The guide draws significantly on work undertaken by Dr Harris for two recent major guidance documents on contaminated land, namely CIRIA's guidance document, *Special Publication 101-112: the remedial treatment of contaminated land* (in press, 1994) and the Welsh Development Agency Manual *Remediation of contaminated land* (November 1993). The importance of these documents is acknowledged by the Institution of Civil Engineers and their publication is warmly welcomed.

Preface

The Department of the Environment's March 1994 consultation paper 'Paying for our Past', which summarises the current policy, legal and regulatory framework for contamination, reiterates the Government's intention that any unacceptable risks to health or the environment from contamination should be dealt with, taking into account the actual or intended use of the land. This 'suitable for use approach' to dealing with situations where damage has occurred from contamination, and the controls in place over actions which may cause future harm to human health or the environment are consistent with the principle of sustainable development.

This design and practice guide on *Contaminated land* addresses the topics of investigation, assessment and remediation of contamination in the context of current thinking on how best to deal with the issues surrounding contaminated land, both in terms of redevelopment and from considerations of human health and environmental impacts. The guide concentrates principally on issues related to chemical contamination of land and water, although reference is made to gases. More specialised matters such as contamination by radioactivity or by explosives are not addressed.

The guide intentionally provides only an overview of what is a very complex subject and draws heavily on authoritative and comprehensive technical guidance documents prepared by bodies such as CIRIA, including *SP101-112: the remedial treatment of contaminated land* (in press, 1994) and those dealing with methane and related in-ground gases.

Although a substantial body of knowledge and practical experience already exists in the UK on contaminated land, much of this derives from the reclamation of derelict sites where contamination has been seen as an additional constraint on development. Historically, contaminated land has not been a principal focus of reclamation or redevelopment projects. However, recent changes in the legislative and policy framework and a growing social awareness of the issues, require the use of a targeted, rational and structured approach to dealing with contaminated land, which is best provided by a risk management framework.

Many of the techniques of investigation used for contaminated or potentially contaminated land are well known and considerable experience exists on their use among geotechnical and civil engineering professionals. Part I of the guide sets the use of these methods within a risk management context and highlights those aspects where different techniques or a different emphasis is needed to ensure that contamination is adequately addressed. The guide describes risk assessment as a means of evaluating the significance of any contamination identified, and emphasises the importance of determining plausible hazard–pathway–target scenarios as part of the assessment process.

Within a risk management framework, remedial methods aim to reduce the identified risks to acceptable levels. Part II of the guide addresses setting objectives for remediation, such as acceptable residual concentrations of contaminants (Contamination Related Objectives), and the overall selection process to determine the most appropriate remedial strategy to achieve the required objectives.

Methods traditionally used to reclaim derelict land have involved civil engineering techniques. Their use has been extended into contaminated land applications with considerable success. The techniques are generally well known and commercially available at competitive prices. However, these methods do not destroy, modify or eliminate the contaminated material and hence attention has turned over recent years to process-based techniques which offer the possibility of solving the problems of contamination more 'permanently'. There is increasing availability of and familiarity with these techniques in the UK, although, as yet, not widespread application. Process-based methods can offer benefits over traditional civil engineering techniques but tend to be more specialised in their application and hence not appropriate in every case.

Dealing with contaminated land requires a multi-disciplinary approach and the use of appropriately experienced specialists is vital to achieving cost effective and technically sufficient investigation, assessment and remediation. Use of technical guidance documents such as this are no substitute for specialist expertise.

Contents

5. Remedial options

6. Remedy selection

7. Design and implementation

Appendices

Part I Investigation and assessment

1. Introduction

What is contaminated land?

Contaminated land has not been officially defined in the UK. However, one definition produced by an international working group (the NATO Committee on Challenges to Modern Society (CCMS) pilot study group)[1] provides a useful starting point (see Box 1.1).

Box 1.1 NATO/CCMS definition of contaminated land

> 'Land that contains substances which, when present in sufficient quantities or concentrations, are likely to cause harm, directly or indirectly, to man, to the environment, or on occasion to other targets.'

This definition broadly embraces most international perspectives of contaminated land, although in UK practice only land containing substances of non-natural origin would be considered as contaminated land: land containing contaminants, such as radon, which are naturally present would generally be excluded.

In the UK, actual or potential contamination is normally considered in the context of redevelopment. Thus, efforts will usually be made to investigate land that has been used for industrial or other purposes to determine whether it is contaminated, and what action (if any) needs to be taken to permit its safe re-use for another purpose. Land which is not subject to redevelopment (e.g. because it is already in industrial use) may also contain contaminants that pose potential health or environmental risks. Action may be taken to investigate, assess and remediate such land where required. However, the basis for assessing the risks associated with land in operational use, and the practical and time constraints on investigation and remediation, will usually be very different to those applying to a typical redevelopment scheme.[2]

A wide range of industrial and other activities have been shown to be associated with contaminated land.[2] A number of well known examples are given in Box 1.2.

In addition to industrial uses of the type detailed in Box 1.2, contamination can be found associated with local cottage industries or activities, for example the presence of deposits of mercury waste in the garden of a building where dentistry had been practised, and also with agricultural procedures such as the use of pesticides.

It is important to be aware that sites adjacent, or close to these industries or activities may have been contaminated through such processes as atmospheric deposition, dust blow and the migration of contaminants in surface and ground-water. The potential for contamination is therefore not confined to the direct use of a site; it may reflect the impact of neighbouring uses or activities.

Box 1.2 Industries and activities known to be associated with contaminated land

- Asbestos manufacture and use
- Chemical industries
- Dockyards
- Explosive manufacture
- Gas and electricity supply industries
- Iron and steel works
- Metal smelting and refining
- Metal treatment and finishing
- Mining and extraction
- Oil refining, distribution and storage
- Paints and graphics
- Pharmaceutical industries
- Scrap processing industries
- Sewage works and farms
- Tanning and associated trades
- Transport industries
- Use of radioactive substances
- Waste disposal operations
- Wood preserving

Why is contaminated land a potential problem?

The UK has a long industrial history and many sites have been damaged as a result of their former use. Physical damage may be evident in the form of unstable ground, poor drainage, underground obstacles, voids and shafts, and topographical irregularities. Such features may pose problems for redevelopment or affect the aesthetic value of a site. Some may represent significant physical hazards, e.g. unstable ground or voids susceptible to collapse. However, where land is con-taminated the main concern is that substances are present which may pose sig-nificant risks to human health or the environment due to their toxicological or other hazardous properties. Humans potentially at risk from contaminative sub-stances may include investigation personnel and construction workers, as well as site users and the general public.

Hazardous substances and materials that may be encountered on contaminated sites include those listed in Table 1.1.[2] One recent Construction Industry Research and Information Association (CIRIA) publication[3] includes examples of the types of contaminative hazards which would be expected in relation to different former uses of a site, and the Building Research Establishment (BRE) are currently preparing (under contract to the Department of the Envi-ronment) typical profiles for different potentially contaminating land uses.

A hazard is a property or situation that has the potential to cause harm. Hazards may be chemical (e.g. the presence of a potentially carcinogenic substance), bio-logical (presence of a pathological bacterium) or physical (accumulation of an explosive or flammable gas). A risk is the probability that harm will occur. Harm may be damage to human health, other living organisms, environmental quality (e.g. of air, water etc.), or physical structures such as buildings or services.

In a wider context, risks may be considered in terms of damage to financial interests and assets. Thus, site owners may take steps to limit potential envi-ronmental liabilities, and increase the commercial value of their assets, by investigating and remediating contaminated sites where appropriate. Potential purchasers will be concerned to avoid exposure to the same liabilities (and associated costs) through the acquisition of contaminated land and property.

Therefore land contamination becomes an issue of concern in relation to the risks it poses. The presence of measurable concentrations of chemicals in the ground does not automatically indicate that there is a contamination problem.

The risks associated with contaminated land should be always be assessed in terms of pathways (the route by which a hazard comes into contact with a target) and targets (the entity that could be harmed through contact with a hazard). It is important to remember that a risk does not exist unless there is a plausible hazard–pathway–target relationship. Examples of hazards, pathways and targets which may be relevant in contaminated land applications are shown in Figure 1.

The degree of risk, and whether it is sufficiently serious to warrant action, depends primarily on the nature of the hazard–pathway–target relationship. Much of the practical effort of investigating, assessing and, where necessary, remediating contaminated land is therefore geared towards:

— identifying and characterising plausible hazard–pathway–target relationships
— establishing the nature and magnitude of the risks and associated effects
— deciding whether the risks are acceptable and, if they are not,
— deciding the best way of controlling or reducing the risks to an acceptable level, taking into account any practical, financial or other constraints
— planning, designing and implementing remedial action and demonstrating that it has been effective.

For contaminated land it is now accepted[2,4,5] that this process is best handled within a formal risk management framework.

Table 1.1 Hazardous substances and materials that may be encountered on a contaminated site

General category	Examples
Toxic, narcotic and otherwise harmful gases and vapours	Carbon dioxide, carbon monoxide, hydrogen sulphide, hydrogen cyanide, toluene, benzene
Flammable and explosive gases	Acetylene, butane, hydrogen sulphide, hydrogen, methane, petroleum hydrocarbons
Flammable liquids and solids	Fuel oils, solvents, process feedstocks, intermediates and products
Combustible materials	Coal residues, ash, timber, variety of domestic, commercial and industrial wastes
Materials liable to self-ignition	Paper, grain, sawdust — if present in large volume and sufficiently damp to initiate microbial degradation

Table 1.1 Hazardous substances and materials that may be encountered on a contaminated site — continued

General category	Examples
Corrosive substances	Acids and alkalis, reactive feedstocks, intermediates and products
Zootoxic metals (and their salts)	Cadmium, lead, mercury, arsenic, beryllium, copper
Other zootoxic chemicals	Pesticides, herbicides
Carcinogenic substances	Asbestos, arsenic, benzene, benzo(a)pyrene
Allergenic substances and sensitisers	Nickel, chromium
Substances causing skin damage	Acids, alkalis, phenols, solvents
Phytotoxic metals	Copper, zinc, nickel, boron
Reactive inorganic salts	Sulphate, cyanide, ammonium, sulphide
Pathogenic agents	Anthrax, polio, tetanus, Weils
Radioactive substances	Some hospital laboratory wastes, radium-contaminated objects and wastes, some mine ore wastes, some non-ferrous slags or phosphorus slags
Physically hazardous materials	Glass, hypodermic syringes
Vermin	Rats, mice, cockroaches

Source: CIRIA SP 101–112[2]

Professional advice

Dealing with contaminated land requires the input of specialists with appropriate experience. Investigation, assessment and remediation of contamination involves a number of disciplines such as chemistry, geology, hydrogeology, geotechnical engineering and civil engineering. It is important that project managers for schemes which involve contaminated land appreciate and act on the need for specialist professionals to be part of the project team. It is not the intention of this guide, nor indeed other authoritative guidance documents such as CIRIA SP 101–112,[2] to provide an alternative to the use of appropriately experienced experts.

*Figure 1 Examples
of hazards, pathways
and targets*

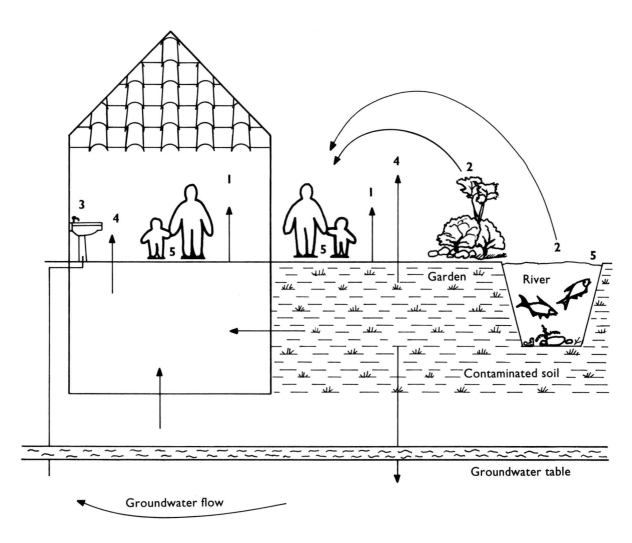

Possible pathways

Ingestion: of contaminated soil/dust [1]
                of contaminated food [2]
                of contaminated water [3]

Inhalation: of contaminated soil particles/dust/vapours [4]

Direct contact: with contaminated soil/dust or water [5]

2. The risk management framework

Scope

The Royal Society definition[6] of risk management is shown in Box 2.1.

Box 2.1 Definition of risk management

> 'The process whereby decisions are made to accept a known or assessed risk and/or the implementation of actions to reduce the consequences or probabilities of occurrence.'

The main advantages of a risk management approach to contaminated land are that:

— it is systematic and objective
— it specifically provides for the assessment of uncertainty
— it provides a rational, consistent, transparent and defensible basis for discussion about a proposed course of action between the relevant parties (e.g. site owner, advisors, regulatory authorities, the local community).

There are four main elements:

(a) hazard identification and assessment
(b) risk estimation
(c) risk evaluation
(d) risk control.

Hazard identification and assessment, risk estimation and risk evaluation together comprise risk assessment; risk evaluation and risk control together comprise risk reduction.

The relationship between risk management and the main stages of a work programme of site investigation, assessment and remediation are shown in Figure 2. Although it is convenient to present the various components of risk management, and associated work activities, as discrete steps there is considerable scope for iteration throughout the entire process. Iteration is in fact an essential feature of most contaminated land work because it allows:

— better targeting of effort
— more accurate definition of the problem and possible solutions
— better technical and financial control over all associated programmes of work.

Figure 2 Relationship between risk management and main stages of a work programme

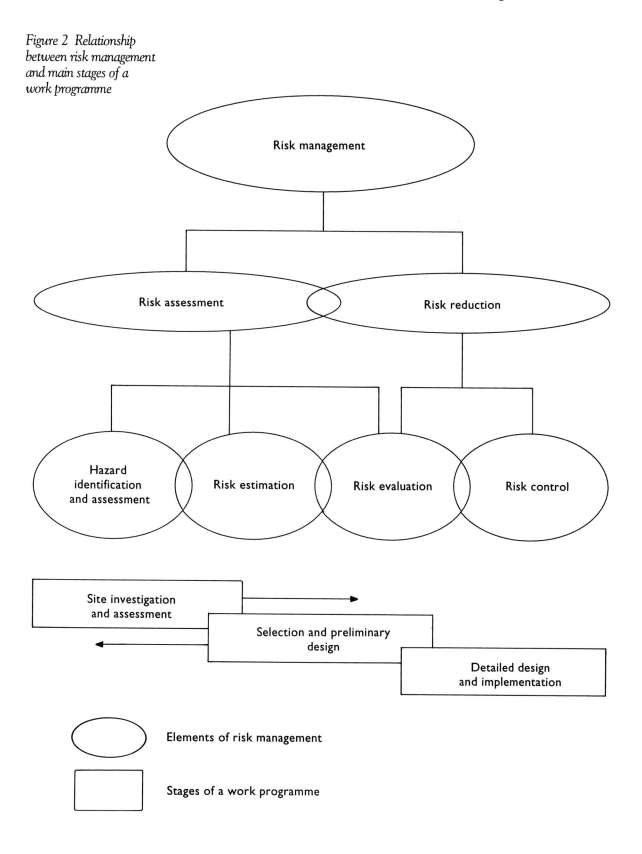

Risk assessment   Risk assessment is that part of risk management which comprises appraisal of the significance of observed levels of contamination on a site. This requires the contaminative hazards and risks to be identified and characterised, and their significance evaluated with respect to the relevant targets. There are two main approaches.

(a) The use of hazard identification and assessment, where judgements are based on the outcome of a comparison between observed levels of contamination and generic reference data indicative of specific types and level of risk. This provides a measure of the *potential* for harm — no attempt is made to estimate the probability that harm will occur. Examples of generic reference data include ICRCL trigger concentration values for soils[7] and Waste Management Paper 27 values for soil gas.[8]

(b) The use of site-specific risk estimation and evaluation where some attempt is made to estimate the probability that harm will occur under the individual circumstances being considered: risk estimates may be qualitative (e.g. the risk is high, medium or low) or quantitative (e.g. the risk of a defined level of harm is less than 1 in 10^6).

The two approaches are not mutually exclusive. For example, a hazard assessment may be carried out initially, with more detailed risk estimation/risk evaluation restricted to those contaminants where generic reference data are not available or where significant risks are likely to be involved. However, a full site-specific risk assessment leading to a quantified estimate of risk to defined targets is a lengthy and complex procedure which is unlikely to be justified or economic except in highly specific circumstances, such as:

— when dealing with particularly complex problems
— when a site in existing use appears to present significant health and/or environmental risks
— when public perception is such that quantified estimates have to be produced.

In practice, and for most redevelopment applications, hazard assessment or qualitative risk estimation are likely to be sufficient to decide the significance of observed levels of contamination and the most appropriate way forward. However, the use of available generic guidelines or standards still requires identification of susceptible targets and evaluation of plausible hazard–pathway–target scenarios, as part of the hazard assessment approach.

Risk reduction   Risk reduction is that part of risk management in which:

— it is decided that observed levels of contamination pose unacceptable risks to defined targets
— risk reduction/control objectives are identified
— decisions are made on the type of response needed to control or reduce risks to a defined level
— a remedial strategy is developed and put into effect
— monitoring procedures are put into place to ensure that both the short- and long-term objectives of remedial action are achieved.

There will usually be several remedial options available; each will have different implications in terms of:

— technical effectiveness (including over the long term) in controlling/reducing risks to the required level
— feasibility (in terms of meeting other technical objectives, such as engineering properties, availability of necessary skills, plant, support services, time, minimal environmental impacts etc.)
— acceptability to relevant parties
— cost.

For the redevelopment of a contaminated site in the UK, the risk reduction/control objectives will take the form of agreed remedial standards, otherwise termed here Contamination Related Objectives (CROs), which take into account the proposed use of the site. These are normally expressed as residual concentrations of contaminants in affected media (soils, groundwaters, surface waters etc.) that are considered acceptable following remedial action. Examples of CROs are listed in Box 2.2.

Box 2.2 Examples of CROs

- The concentrations of specified contaminants that should not be exceeded in soils remaining in place following excavation
- The concentrations of specified contaminants that should not be exceeded in recycled/imported replacement materials
- The concentration of specified contaminants present in the coarse clean fraction of a soils washing plant
- The concentration of contaminants present in groundwater following a pump-to-treat operation
- The concentration of contaminants in groundwater on the 'clean' side of a cement-bentonite cut-off wall

Typically, CROs will be more stringent where the site is required for residential or horticultural use as opposed, for example, to hard cover, commercial or industrial use.

Although the phrase 'clean-up' standards or values is commonly used to denote the CROs, this usage is not supported because it may be misleading where there is no formal definition of 'clean' and where a risk assessment may show different residual concentrations of contaminants to be acceptable under different site conditions.

Remedial action may also be required to meet other technical objectives (e.g. to achieve appropriate site levels, a suitable base for construction, areas for landscape), and be practical and economic. While CROs should take priority in arriving at decisions on the type of remedial action to be taken, in practice it may be difficult to reconcile all the technical objectives of a scheme and overcome all associated practical and cost constraints. One of the aims of risk reduction/control is therefore to select that remedial strategy which offers the greatest scope for controlling/reducing risks and meeting other technical objectives, while at the same time minimising practical problems and costs.

If it proves impossible to meet objectives and overcome constraints it may be necessary to re-evaluate the basis for action or adjust certain aspects of the scheme. For example it may be necessary to:

— adopt a different use of the site (in which case it may be possible to redefine CROs)
— allow more time for completion of remedial action
— provide more resources to overcome short- and long-term constraints.

Communication aspects

The communication of risk-based information to third parties is an important element of all stages of risk management. It requires particular care to ensure that information is accurately and appropriately presented and that it results in well-informed and constructive interaction. Examples of the types of issues that should be addressed when considering how information about contaminated land should be communicated are listed in Box 2.3. For the reasons noted above, use of the terms 'clean' or 'clean-up' in contaminated land applications is not recommended.

Box 2.3 Communication issues

Issues to be addressed	**Types of information**
• Degree and nature of involvement	• Site investigation data
• Nature of concern and perception of risks	• Risk assessment findings
• Types of information to be communicated	• Remedial design proposals and method statements
• Frequency of communication	• Monitoring proposals and findings
• Presentational requirements	• Validation proposals and findings
• Available channels	• Post-treatment management programme and findings
Possible party	**Possible methods and procedures**
• Regulators	• Written reports
• Funders	• Oral presentations
• Insurers	• Liaison meetings
• Neighbours	• Site visits
• Local community	• Contact points
• Local councillors	

In some circumstances there may be a legal requirement for formal liaison, site access and information disclosure, for example:

— with a local planning authority in accordance with the conditions of a planning permission or obligation
— with the National Rivers Authority in relation to liquid discharges to a controlled water
— with a waste regulation authority in relation to contaminated material designated for off-site disposal.

3. Site investigation and risk assessment

Introduction

Site investigation and assessment are critically important in the effective risk management of contaminated land. Site investigation and assessment findings provide the basis for decisions on the need for, and type of, remedial action and, ultimately, for the design and implementation of the necessary works. Deficiencies in site investigation and assessment could lead to errors of judgement, and may affect the technical sufficiency, cost and duration of remedial action for contaminated land projects as with all investigations for construction schemes.[9] Poorly informed and executed site investigation works may also expose investigation personnel, and the general public, to unacceptable health risks and could lead to more extensive or intractable contamination problems than those which previously existed on the site. A multi-disciplinary approach is especially important for investigations into contamination, and project managers should ensure that the investigation team includes appropriately skilled professionals covering geology, chemistry, hydrogeology and geotechnics, together with other disciplines as needed for the particular scheme.

Site investigation

Purpose

The overall purpose of site investigation is to ensure that an appropriate information base exists for assessing and managing the risks that may be associated with contaminated land. Since site investigation effectively underpins all the decisions and actions subsequently taken in connection with a contaminated site, it is essential that:

— it is properly designed and executed by appropriately skilled personnel
— it provides information that can be interpreted by means of a risk assessment, that is, it must address all relevant potential hazards, pathways and targets
— it poses minimal risks to site personnel, the general public and the wider environment.

Investigation also requires access to the site and, in its later stages, typically involves physical disturbance of the ground. In some circumstances site-based work may necessitate prior approval from the regulatory authorities (see Legal aspects, below): it is essential that this is in place before site work begins.

Adequate investigation and assessment also require time. The lack of sufficient time during the planning stages of a project is one of the main factors limiting the effectiveness of the risk assessment process. Professional advisors should make every effort to explain to their clients any significance of time constraints with respect to the particular circumstances of an individual project.

Scope and objectives

Defining the scale and nature of any contamination present on the site is clearly a key objective of site investigation. However, it is not sufficient in itself to permit an adequate assessment of risks. As indicated in Chapter 2, this requires that all potential pathways and targets, including those associated with the off-site migration of contaminants, are properly identified and defined.

In addition to contamination aspects, therefore, the investigation must address the geological and hydrological properties of the site since these affect the behaviour of contaminants in the environment and may have a bearing on potential targets (e.g. the water environment may provide a migratory pathway or itself represent a target at risk of harm; foreseeable events such as flooding could affect the distribution of contaminants and the targets at risk). Investigation work may also have to extend beyond site boundaries because targets at most risk may be located at some distance away from the site.

The aim should therefore be to address four main aspects (see Table 3.1):

— contamination
— geology (including geotechnical aspects)
— hydrology (including both surface and groundwater)
— pathways and targets.

Since site investigation can be a lengthy and expensive process, and there is obvious synergy between the different aspects, it is sensible to develop an investigation strategy which addresses all four aspects on an integrated basis.

Table 3.1 Aspects to be considered during the investigation of contaminated sites

Aspect	Rationale
Contamination	Provides information on potential hazards: information requirements include nature (e.g. chemical/physical form etc.), extent and distribution (on and off site) of the contaminant(s)
Geology	Provides data on the physical characteristics of the ground and of contaminated media: these may affect the location and behaviour of contaminants (e.g. adsorption onto clay/organic matter; migration via underground mineworkings) and the type of remedial action that can be taken (e.g. implications of underground obstacles, services, potential for subsidence during dewatering etc.)
Hydrology	Provides information on sensitivity of potential water targets (e.g. streams, rivers, lakes, groundwater) and likely transport and fate of contaminants in the water environment
Pathways and targets	Fundamental in determining whether there is a risk of harm (i.e. whether plausible hazard–pathway–target scenarios exist), and the magnitude and severity of the risk(s) in relation to existing and likely future conditions

Site investigation is also required to meet a wide range of other practical information needs, from establishing the health and safety requirements of investigation and remediation personnel to identifying any factors that may affect the feasibility of taking particular types of remedial action. Specific objectives (such as those listed in Box 3.1) should therefore be developed to assist in the design and implementation of site investigation work.[2]

Box 3.1 Typical objectives for investigation of contamination

- To determine the nature and extent of any contamination of soils and groundwater on the site
- To determine the nature and extent of any contamination migrating off the site into neighbouring soils and groundwater
- To determine the nature and engineering implications of other hazards and features on the site (e.g. expansive slags, combustibility, deep foundations, storage tanks)
- To identify, characterise and assess potential targets and likely pathways
- To provide sufficient information (including a reference level to judge effectiveness) to identify and evaluate alternative remedial strategies
- To determine the need for, and scope of, both short- and long-term monitoring and maintenance
- To formulate safe site working practices and ensure effective protection of the environment during remedial works
- To identify and plan for immediate human health and environmental protection and contingencies for any emergency action

Main phases of investigation

At the outset it is clearly not economic or feasible to examine in detail all areas of a site or to test for all possible contaminants. However, at the beginning of an investigation it is rarely apparent what the main priorities should be. Specific health and safety, and environmental protection requirements, are also unlikely to be known with certainty. Phasing offers a valuable means of identifying and refining site investigation priorities, ensuring safe working practices, and minimising costs by allowing for successive cycles of data gathering and evaluation.

The investigation of contaminated sites should involve at least three phases (preliminary, detailed and compliance/performance investigations) and may involve up to five:

(a) preliminary investigation (comprising desk study and site reconnaissance)
(b) exploratory investigation (e.g. preliminary sampling, monitoring)
(c) detailed investigation (involving detailed on-site exploratory work)
(d) supplementary investigation (the collection of additional site investigation data for specified purposes)
(e) investigation for compliance and performance (comprising on-going monitoring and validation of remedial action, and post-treatment management).

There is scope for overlap between these phases. For example, some initial exploratory work (e.g. sampling and analysis of surface deposits) may be combined with site reconnaissance; supplementary investigation may form the final stage of an extended main site investigation. However, site investigation personnel should not enter a site, and no initial exploratory work should be carried out, unless and until a desk study has indicated that it is safe to do so. The desk study will also provide the information necessary to determine appropriate health and safety precautions for the investigation personnel undertaking subsequent phases. For example, the British Drilling Association/Institution of Civil Engineers classification system for potentially contaminated sites for drilling purposes[10] utilises such information.

Environmental protection needs, such as not siting a borehole or extending it to such depth that the borehole itself provides a pathway for contaminant migration, may influence the investigation phasing. For example, the exploratory investigation phase may be used to obtain sufficient information to allow safe borehole location in critical areas or to assist judgements on the depth to be investigated.

Each phase in the investigation of a contaminated site has a different set of objectives, and involves different types of activity (see Table 3.2). It is important to note that the findings of each phase are used as the basis for designing the next. Thus, a preliminary site investigation report should set out the conclusions drawn from the work, and a series of objectives and plans for the next phase.

For economic and data interpretation reasons, the aim should be to conduct an integrated investigation so that all four main aspects of contamination, geology, hydrology and pathways/targets can be addressed at the same time. However, the extent to which this can be achieved in practice varies depending on the phase of the investigation.

Integration of the preliminary investigation should pose the least difficulty, although different reference data should be consulted during the desk study (see Appendix A for typical information sources on contamination and hydrological aspects). However, during the main and supplementary phases of site investigation, specific provision (e.g. siting of boreholes, wells, trial pits, numbers and types of samples collected etc.) may have to be made to gather information on different aspects, for example for geotechnical purposes as well as contamination objectives. See Box 3.2 for an example of potential conflict between investigation objectives on risk assessment and those relating to construction.

Box 3.2 Example of possible conflict between site investigation objectives

- It may be necessary to sink a borehole to determine the contamination and hydrogeological properties of a site at depth. The borehole may be sited with the intention of installing a permanent groundwater monitoring well as part of a wider network monitoring groundwater quality over the long term. Siting decisions will be governed by what is already known, or anticipated, about regional and site-specific hydrogeological properties, the likely behaviour of the contaminants at depth and the specific role of the well as part of a wider network.
- The data collected from the installation and operation of the well may be useful in the design of any planned construction on the site. However, siting, construction and operating parameters should be determined by contamination/hydrogeological objectives and not by construction needs (e.g. to determine the bearing capacity of the ground in a specific location). A separate borehole should be sunk to satisfy these additional requirements if they conflict with the contamination/hydrogeological objectives, but the data collected from all exploratory holes should be made available to all professional advisors.

Table 3.2 *Examples of objectives and activities associated with site investigation*

Phase of investigation	Typical objectives	Typical activities
Preliminary investigation	To provide background information on past and current uses, hazards, geology and hydrology, possible scale of contamination etc. To inform design of on-site work (including sampling and analysis, health and safety, environmental protection) Can be used to rank a number of sites based on hazard potential May provide initial indication of remedial needs	Literature review Consultation (e.g. site owners, neighbours, regulatory authorities) Site visits
Exploratory investigation	To confirm initial hypotheses about contamination and site characteristics To refine design of detailed investigation	Preliminary sampling (e.g. surface deposits, vegetation) Preliminary monitoring (e.g. gas composition and groundwater quality, flora and fauna)
Detailed investigation	To characterise fully contaminants, geology, hydrology of site and associated pathways and targets To inform risk assessment and selection of remedial methods	Comprehensive investigation of ground (e.g. using trial pits, trenches, boreholes) Monitoring (e.g. gas composition and water quality, flora and fauna)
Supplementary investigation	To obtain additional information in support of risk assessment and/or selection of remedial strategies	Further ground investigation and monitoring Treatability testing
Investigation for compliance and performance	To confirm effectiveness of remedial action	Post-treatment validation and monitoring as appropriate

Investigation techniques

A wide range of techniques are available for characterising the contamination, geological, and hydrological profile of a contaminated site. Each has advantages and limitations that must be addressed on a site-specific basis at an early stage in the design of an investigation (see Appendix B, and references 2, 11–14, for further information on available methods and applications).

Different techniques have different implications for:

— the quality and interpretation of site investigation data
— the health and safety of site personnel and the general public
— environmental quality.

For example, rotary drilling in contaminated ground may affect the distribution of volatile contaminants in the formation being sampled and may pose potential hazards to the workforce and the general public if it produces hazardous particulates and gases. Cable percussive boring may similarly affect the distribution of contaminants, can make accurate depth identification for sampling of specific materials difficult and can also pose significant potential hazards to the investigation personnel. The failure to take appropriate precautions when sinking a borehole to significant depth at a site overlying a sensitive aquifer where potentially mobile chlorinated solvents are present, is likely to make an already difficult problem considerably worse.

Appropriate techniques must be selected on the basis of the objectives of the particular phase of the investigation, the geological and hydrogeological conditions and the known or suspected contaminants present. For example, very different techniques would be used for the investigation of potentially combustible material (including those to determine in-situ density, air permeability and temperature throughout the material, and the 'combustion potential', while minimising heat generation or sparks from the investigation techniques themselves) compared with a site thought to contain significant concentrations of heavy metals (where suitable techniques for obtaining representative soil samples for laboratory analyses would be required).

Sampling, analysis and on-site testing

Sampling, analysis and on-site testing strategies must be developed for:

— initial exploratory investigations
— main site investigations
— supplementary investigations
— validation exercises
— monitoring programmes.

It is clearly not possible to collect an infinite number of samples or to test for unlimited numbers of contaminants. In keeping with the overall approach to site investigation, sampling, testing and analysis strategies must be developed according to the specific objectives of each phase, taking into account what is already known about the site. Typical issues to be addressed when developing sampling and analysis strategies are listed in Box 3.3. More detailed information and guidance is available in references 2, 11 and 15.

Box 3.3 Typical issues to be addressed when developing sampling and analysis strategies

Sampling
- What types of samples should be collected (e.g. soils, waters, wastes, gas/air, vegetation)?
- What sampling pattern should be employed?
- How many samples should be collected (across the site and with depth)?
- How much sample should be collected?

Box 3.3 Typical issues to be addressed when developing sampling and analysis strategies — continued

> - How often should samples be collected (over time)?
> - How should samples be collected?
> - How should samples be stored?
> - How should samples be transported?
>
> **Analysis and on-site testing**
>
> - What types of analysis/testing should be conducted (e.g. chemical, biological, physical)?
> - How should samples be prepared for analysis (e.g. no preparation, drying, grinding, sieving)?
> - What level of detection is required?
> - What level of precision is necessary?
> - What analytical testing techniques should be used?
> - How should the data be reported?
> - How quickly are the data needed?
>
> **General**
>
> - What quality assurance/quality control procedures should be applied to ensure the validity of the results (e.g. use of NAMAS[*] accredited laboratories)?

* National Measurement Accreditation Service

A phased approach to sampling and analysis offers similar benefits to a phased approach to site investigation as a whole. It allows for the gradual accumulation of information on the types and location of contaminants present on the site, and the progressive refinement of sampling and analysis objectives and procedures. There are several ways in which phasing can be achieved in practice (see Box 3.4). Further refinements, focusing, for example, on particular areas or materials of concern, or the use of more sensitive, substance-specific analyses, can then be made on the basis of initial findings.

Box 3.4 Examples of a phased approach to sampling and analysis

> - Initial requirements can be established by desk study of the past and current uses of the site; the types of materials (e.g. as raw materials, products, by-products and wastes) stored, used or otherwise handled on the site; and details on the location of process plant, waste disposal and storage areas etc.
> - Background information on the geological/hydrological characteristics of the site, combined with data on the likely behaviour of contaminants in the environment, can be used as a guide to sampling locations/frequencies
> - Field observation (e.g. visual and olfactory) can be used to select appropriate samples for analysis
> - Samples collected in the field can be retained for analysis at a later date (provided this is compatible with storage and sample preparation constraints)
> - Analytical screening techniques, such as Inductively Coupled Plasma and Gas Chromatography/Mass Spectroscopy can also be used to provide a broad indication of the types and approximate quantities of different substances present on the site

The development of sampling and analysis strategies is highly site-specific and is still to a large extent guided by the experience and specialist expertise of site investigators and laboratory personnel. While 'judgemental' sampling and analysis is extremely valuable, in terms of increasing the efficiency and minimising the cost of site investigation, it should not be regarded as a substitute for a thorough and statistically sound approach.

Research has recently been published on the statistical basis for sampling contaminated land.[16] This has confirmed the importance of some form of systematic grid for locating sampling positions across a site. Statistically based regular grid sampling is useful because it can define the lateral boundaries of contamination (such as a 'hot spot') with a specified degree of confidence. However, it is important to remember that contaminant distributions may vary significantly with depth and sampling positions and frequencies must be sufficient to define the vertical extent of contamination (e.g. by collecting samples below the level at which visual or other information on the anticipated behaviour of the contaminant suggests contamination is unlikely to be present). The selection of grid size must be a matter for professional judgement based on the site characteristics and the investigation objectives. For example, the use of a 25 m grid for sampling might be considered too onerous in some circumstances but not in others, such as a modern housing development, where 25 m between exploratory hole locations might mean that only one garden in four is sampled (the average width of a modern terraced house being about 6 m).

In general, it is easier to show that a site is contaminated than to prove that it is uncontaminated.[2] Whatever sampling strategy is adopted therefore, it must be sufficient to demonstrate unequivocally which parts of the site are unaffected (and can therefore be safely excluded from any remedial programme) even if this means extending the sampling and analysis programme beyond that required simply to show the presence of contamination.

Legal aspects

Depending on the exact circumstances, site investigation works may be subject to prior authorisation by the regulatory authorities. Other requirements may have to be satisfied by virtue of the health and safety implications of the work.

Table 3.3 gives brief guidance on the legal provisions that may apply on a site-specific basis. More detailed information on the legislative framework applying to contaminated land can be found in reference 2. Note that the guidance in Table 3.3 applies to the situation in England and Wales (different provisions apply in Scotland and Northern Ireland in some cases, as detailed in reference 2) and that the legislative framework may change from time to time. Appropriate legal advice should always be sought in relation to individual sites.

Health and safety aspects

On-site investigation work (including site reconnaissance) may expose personnel to health and safety risks. Hazards may relate to substances (solids, liquids, gases) present on the site (above and below ground) or to its physical condition (e.g. unsound buildings or other structures, voids, unstable ground etc.). Physical injuries (e.g. cuts, grazes) may enhance the risks associated with exposure to hazardous substances by creating a ready means of access into the body. The possible significance of health and safety issues is much greater for an investigation into potentially contaminated land than for a conventional geotechnical investigation. The development of appropriate health and safety provisions is therefore a vital aspect of the design of any investigation of a contaminated site, and site reconnaisance or inspection visits should not be made without proper consideration of the risks to the personnel involved or to the general public.

Site investigation work is subject to health and safety legislation including the *Control of Substances Hazardous to Health (COSHH) Regulations 1988*. These require an assessment to be made of all relevant health risks before a work activity commences, and the use of appropriate control measures where necessary. The *Management of Health and Safety at Work etc. Regulations 1992* extend the assessment to cover all types of hazards and hazardous activities, and include the welfare of the general public. The forthcoming *Construction (Design and Management) Regulations* require that consultants and specifiers ensure that their designs can be constructed satisfactorily. This will apply to the design of remedial works and other construction works on contaminated land as well as to matters of general engineering design.

Table 3.3 Legal provisions that may apply to site investigation in England and Wales

Area of law	Legal provision	Requirement
Land use planning and development control	Town and Country Planning legislation	Permission for development (which may include site investigation/ monitoring operations in some circumstances)
Public health	Environmental Protection Act 1990	Obligation to prevent the creation of a statutory nuisance (e.g. generation of toxic vapours, dusts etc.)
	Occupier Liability legislation	Obligation to ensure the safety of visitors (which may include trespassers) to premises
Health and safety	Health and Safety at Work etc. Act 1974 and associated regulations	Obligation to protect the health and safety of employees and the general public from hazards arising at a place of work
Environmental protection: Air	Control of Pollution Act 1974	Powers to local authorities to make enquiries about air pollution from any premises, except private dwellings
Water	Water Resources Act 1991	Prior authorisation required from National Rivers Authority (NRA) to make a discharge of polluting substances to a controlled water Powers to NRA to protect the aqueous environment and to remedy or forestall pollution of controlled waters
	Water Industry Act 1991	Prior authorisation required from the sewerage undertaker to make a discharge of polluting material to a sewer

*Table 3.3 Legal provisions that may apply to site investigation in England and Wales —
continued*

Area of law	Legal provision	Requirement
Waste	Environmental Protection Act 1990	Duty of Care on all those involved in the production, handling and disposal of controlled waste (e.g. spoil arising from trial pit/borehole) to ensure that they follow safe, authorised, and properly documented procedures and practices
Protected areas, species and artifacts	Town and Country Planning Act, 1990; Wildlife and Countryside Act, 1981; Ancient Monuments and Archaeological Areas Act, 1979	Protection of designated areas (e.g. Sites of Special Scientific Interest), species (e.g. plants and animals) and artifacts (e.g. ancient monuments)

Specific requirements will vary depending on the nature of the site and the phase of investigation. Typical issues to be addressed when developing health and safety plans are listed in Box 3.5.

Box 3.5 Health and safety issues

Health and safety procedures

- Controlled entry (permit to work) procedures (where applicable)
- Site zoning (i.e. 'dirty' and clean areas)
- Good hygiene (e.g. no smoking, eating except in designated areas)
- Monitoring (e.g. for on-, off-site toxic/hazardous gases)
- Appropriate disposal of wastes
- Safe handling, storage and transport of hazardous samples
- Control of nuisance (e.g. noise, vibration, dust and odour)
- Emergency procedures
- Provision of appropriate training (e.g. to recognise hazards, use equipment)
- Need for routine health surveillance

Health and safety equipment

- Washing and eating facilities
- Protective clothing (e.g. for eyes, head, hands and feet)
- Monitoring equipment (e.g. personal exposure, ambient concentrations)
- Respiratory equipment
- First aid box
- Telephone link
- Decontamination facilities (e.g. for boots, clothing, machinery)

More detailed information and guidance on health and safety provision during the investigation of contaminated sites is available elsewhere.[3,10,17]

Quality assurance and control

Quality assurance/quality control (QA/QC) in site investigation and assessment is an important means of confirming the validity of the procedures and data used for risk assessment purposes. Aspects of site investigation and assessment that could be subject to QA/QC procedures include those listed in Box 3.6.

Box 3.6 QA/QC for site investigation and risk assessment

- Compliance with all relevant legal requirements
- Review of documentary evidence during desk study
- Location and recording of observations during site reconnaissance
- Procedures used to identify potential hazard–pathway–target relationships and to select 'plausible' scenarios for further assessment
- Siting and installation of exploratory excavations
- Establishment and performance of environmental protection measures
- Waste disposal arrangements (Duty of Care etc.)
- Implementation of health and safety procedures
- Collection and handling of samples
- Storage and preparation of samples
- Methods of analysis and testing
- On-site recording protocols
- Reporting of data
- Reporting procedures used in estimation of risks
- Input to, and use of any models to aid interpretation of the data
- Participation by contracting parties in appropriate accreditation schemes (e.g. BS 5750[18] for quality management, NAMAS for analytical and testing services, CONTEST* for analytical proficiency)

* Scheme operated by the Laboratory of the Government Chemist under the DTI's 'Validity of Analytical Measurement' initiative

More detailed information on the use of QA/QC procedures in contaminated land applications, and in sampling and analysis in particular, can be found in reference 2.

Risk assessment

Objectives

The purpose of risk assessment is to determine:

— whether observed levels of contamination on a site are likely to pose unacceptable risks to defined targets now or in the future
— whether measures should be taken to reduce/control risks to an acceptable level.

Specific objectives of risk assessment[2] include those listed in Box 3.7.

Box 3.7 Objectives of risk assessment

- To determine systematically any risks arising from any contamination present on the site and whether these are 'unacceptable'
- To provide, at least, a qualitative statement about the magnitude and nature of the risks where they exist
- To determine the effects of foreseeable events, such as weather extremes, rising water-table, flooding, increase in neighbouring populations etc., on the nature and magnitude of the risks

Box 3.7 Objectives of risk assessment — continued

- To determine the consequences (e.g. potential impacts on the environment, groundwater resources, public health) of a change of use, development, redevelopment or other works on the site
- To identify the critical contaminants and associated factors (e.g. pathways) relevant to the site so that the steps necessary to reduce risks to 'acceptable' levels, both currently and in the foreseeable future, can be determined
- To help to set objectives and priorities for reducing risks
- To make judgements about the significance and acceptability of identified risks
- To provide a rational and defensible basis for discussion about a proposed course of action with third parties, (e.g. regulators, insurers, local community etc.)

Hazard identification and assessment

Hazard identification and assessment involves collecting sufficient information about the contaminants, the site (including its geotechnical and hydrological characteristics), and the wider environment to identify, characterise and assess the importance of hazards, pathways and targets. Hazard identification and assessment is informed by site investigation, initially through desk studies and site reconnaissance, and subsequently through the main site investigation work.

Deciding whether observed levels of contamination are significant in terms of anticipated pathways and targets typically involves the activities listed in Box 3.8. This process should be carried out for each contaminant observed at the site.

Box 3.8 Hazard identification and assessment

- Comparison of observed concentrations with published data on natural 'background' levels of contaminants and/or local background concentrations*
- Qualitative exposure assessment to establish what hazard–pathway–target scenarios exist and which are plausible§
- Comparison of observed concentrations with reference data indicative of negligible risk under defined conditions of exposure

* Comparison with background data should be done with care: observed levels may be lower than background and still represent a hazard under some conditions of exposure.

§ Note that a contaminant may be present at concentrations above background or other reference level and not represent a hazard if there is no pathway by which it can reach a target — for example, high concentrations of insoluble metals located at depth which are not 'available' to targets either through direct contact or migration e.g. through wind or water action.

Both dedicated (derived specifically for the purpose of assessing contaminated land) and non-dedicated generic reference data can be used for assessment purposes. Examples of potentially useful reference data are listed in Table 3.4.

The ICRCL trigger concentration values are guidelines which have been produced by the UK Interdepartmental Committee on the Redevelopment of Contaminated Land as an aid to the assessment of contaminated sites intended for redevelopment (see Box 3.9). The values, and the rationale for their use, can be found in ICRCL Guidance Note 59/83.[7] Additional information on the derivation of trigger concentration values for former coal carbonisation plant is published in a separate report.[32]

Table 3.4 *Examples of generic reference data* for assessment purposes*

Medium	Dedicated[§]	Non-dedicated[†]
Soils	ICRCL trigger concentration values[7] Dutch standards[19] Canadian guidelines[20] Australian/New Zealand guidelines[21]	Application of sewage sludge to land[28]
Water	Dutch[19], Canadian guidelines[20]	Drinking water standards and water quality objectives[29]
Air	—	Air quality standards[30] Occupational Exposure Standards and Maximum Exposure Limits[31]
Soil gas	WMP No. 27 on landfill gas[8] BRE guidance[22] ICRCL guidance on the development and after-use of landfill sites[23] CIRIA guidance on methane[24–26] IP guidance[27]	—

* The term 'reference' value has specific connotations in relation to the Dutch values.
[§] Values have been developed specifically for the assessment of contaminated land.
[†] Values have not been developed specifically for this application but may be useful for assessment purposes.

Guidance documents have also been published by ICRCL for other scenarios, and these can be of assistance in appropriate circumstances.

Box 3.9 *The ICRCL trigger concentration values*

- The ICRCL trigger concentration guidelines are intended to assist in the exercise of professional judgement on the significance of contamination on a site intended for development

- Two sets of values are presented for a selection of common soil contaminants and a range of proposed uses:

  (a) The **threshold trigger value** which indicates the concentration above which it may be necessary to carry out additional investigation and/or take some form of remedial action

  (b) The **action trigger value** which indicates the concentration above which it is likely that some form of remedial action will be required (possibly following additional investigation)

- Action trigger concentration values are not available for all contaminants. Where a value is not available one must be derived (through site-specific assessment) or reference made to other sources of guidance

- Each value is indicative of specific hazards, e.g. values for nickel and copper relate only to phytotoxic effects and do not take account of human toxicity (copper) or allergenic (nickel) reactions

Reference values should always be selected and used with care, in full knowledge of the technical, policy and legal context in which they were developed and are intended to be applied. For example the Dutch standards[19] which are frequently referred to for UK projects in situations where the ICRCL values[7] do not address the contaminants in question, where the ICRCL action trigger values are not currently specified, and where groundwater contamination is of relevance, were derived for geological and hydrogeological conditions which differ significantly from those in much of the UK and for use in a legal and policy context which bears little resemblance to that of the UK at the present time. Therefore, their validity for use in the assessment of the significance of contamination on a UK site must be carefully evaluated.

Reference data should also be relevant to the hazard–pathway–target scenario under consideration: for example, values based on ecotoxicological considerations are not applicable to human health assessments. All assumptions, safety factors etc. built into the reference values should be noted and taken into account. Similarly, any modification of a reference value to obtain a valid figure for comparison should also be recorded (e.g. factoring up a water quality objective to take account of anticipated dilution/degradation effects along a migration pathway[28]).

Depending on the outcome, the hazard assessment may indicate that:

— observed levels of contamination are unlikely to pose a risk to specified targets and no further action is required
— further investigation and/or assessment (perhaps involving site-specific risk estimation) is needed before the significance of observed levels of contamination can be properly judged
— levels of contamination are such that there is no doubt as to the need for remedial action.

It should be borne in mind that the acceptability of the contamination is judged solely against the assumptions built into the generic guideline or standard being used. It is fundamentally important that the applicability of these assumptions is assessed for each specific circumstance in order to ensure that the outcome of the hazard assessment is defensible.

Risk estimation

Risk estimation involves detailed evaluation of hazards, pathways and targets to determine:

— the nature of the exposure of the target to the hazard
— the nature of the effects produced under defined levels of exposure
— the probability (expressed in either qualitative or quantitative terms) that adverse effects will occur under defined conditions of exposure.

Before commencing risk estimation, the available data should be evaluated (data evaluation) to ensure that they are sufficient in terms of type, quality and quantity. Risk estimation based on inadequate site investigation data is a waste of time and financial resources. Depending on the reference data used, the output of risk estimation may be expressed in qualitative terms (i.e. a narrative statement that the risk of a defined level of harm is high, medium or low), or numeric terms (e.g. the risk of excess cancer over the lifetime of the individual is less than 1 in 10^6).

Two main procedures are carried out:

(*a*) exposure assessment
(*b*) toxicity assessment.

Box 3.10 lists the type of information and procedures typically used to conduct exposure and toxicity assessments.

Box 3.10 Exposure and toxicity assessments

Exposure assessment

The purpose of exposure assessment is to define (typically using models) the environmental transport and fate of contaminants, taking into account:

- chemical form and physical properties
- characteristics of the host medium (soils, rock, groundwater etc.) and effect on contaminant concentrations along travel pathways
- concentration of contaminants at the source, at points along the travel pathway and at the point of exposure (e.g. ingested by the target)
- rate of movement along the pathway
- amounts, frequency and duration of exposure
- characteristics of exposure route (e.g. ingestion, inhalation, direct contact) that determine how much of the contaminant is taken in by the target
- data limitations

Toxicity assessment

The purpose of toxicity assessment is to determine the effect (e.g. toxicological, carcinogenic, mutagenic, corrosive etc.) of the hazard on the target under the conditions of exposure defined in the exposure assessment. Effects assessments involve a consideration of:

- dose-response relationships, and in particular the nature of the response at No Observable Effect Level (NOEL)
- biological mechanisms regulating responses to different types of substances
- factors affecting response of targets (e.g. gender, age, general health status, species composition, physical properties of the building fabric etc.)
- data limitations

Risk estimation will usually require the use of models (e.g. environmental fate and transport and, less commonly, toxicological models) to quantify the amount of a contaminant travelling from the source (e.g. contaminated soil) to the point of exposure (e.g. ingestion by a child), and from the point of exposure to the point of impact within the body. Calculated doses can then be compared against a suitable reference dose to obtain an estimate of risk. In human health risk assessments, for example, the calculated daily intake of a contaminant can be compared against an 'acceptable daily intake' (ADI) or other reference value (e.g. the Cancer Slope Factor used in US health assessments[33]) that links dose to a probable effect. The ADI value is much lower than other short-term toxicity values currently used in the UK, for certain purposes. For example, Waste Management Paper No. 23[34] discusses toxicity in relation to the definition of Special Wastes and makes use of lowest published lethal dose (LDL$_o$) values and LD$_{50}$ values which refer to the concentration which, in a single dose, results in the death of 50% of the population to which it is administered. Since, in contaminated land risk assessments, the aim is to identify risks to human health which might apply over a period of time, it is appropriate to use acceptable daily intake values rather than lethal dose values.

Whether a qualitative or quantitative risk estimation is undertaken, it will usually involve the manipulation of quantified data describing the movement of the contaminant from the source to the target (see Box 3.11).

Analogous procedures can be developed to cover other types of hazards (e.g. calculation of the concentration of an explosive gas in air, taking into account source concentrations, migration characteristics, and circumstances of exposure).

Box 3.11 Human health risk estimation using acceptable daily intakes

- The anticipated intake of a substance by a child is calculated using the concentration of the substance in the source (e.g. soil) and a range of factors including ingestion rate, fraction ingested, body weight, frequency, duration and period of exposure

- The calculated intake is compared with an acceptable daily intake (below which no adverse effects on health are anticipated) to derive a 'hazard index' (ratio of calculated dose to acceptable dose)

- The risk estimate depends on the value of the hazard index:
  - if the calculated dose is lower than the ADI (hazard index less than 1) it can be assumed that the risk of harm is negligible
  - if the calculated dose equates to a lethal dose (hazard index is substantially greater than 1) then the risk of harm is clearly very high
  - if some intermediate value is obtained, professional judgement must be used to estimate the likely level of risk

Exposure and toxicity assessments are typically subject to many uncertainties due to information gaps in the effects and toxicity assessments. While every effort should be made to reduce uncertainties, for example by collecting more detailed site investigation data, it may be necessary to make assumptions in order to complete an assessment. A common approach is to apply a 'worst case' scenario so that sufficient safety margins are built into the assessment. Some assumptions may be present in the default values built into models. In all cases it is essential to identify and record all uncertainties and assumptions used in the assessment. It is also important to ensure that the assumptions used will stand up to scrutiny and that sensitivity of the risk estimation to the different assumptions involved is properly appreciated.

Risk evaluation

Risk evaluation involves making judgements about the acceptability of risk estimates, having regard to available guidance and taking into account any uncertainties associated with the process. It is important to remember that initial judgements about the acceptability of a risk may be modified at a later date when the costs and feasibility of taking remedial action have been more fully evaluated (see Chapters 4–7). For example, a risk may be considered unacceptable (even when judged to be low) if there are serious consequences (e.g. an explosion leading to human fatalities). A high risk (e.g. death of a proportion of young landscape plants) may be tolerated if the cost and practical problems of removing the source of the risk (moderately high concentrations of phytotoxic metals) are more onerous than those associated with rectifying the damage (e.g. periodic replacement of stock) should it occur. Different parties may also have different views on what constitutes an 'unacceptable' risk.

There is no published UK guidance on the acceptability of the risks associated with contaminated land, although the Health and Safety Executive has published guidance on the tolerability of risks to residents living in the vicinity of hazardous installations.[35] The US Environmental Protection Agency has developed risk acceptability criteria and protocols for use in assessing the human health risks associated with hazardous waste sites[33] but these may not be directly applicable to the UK context. Thus, the risk evaluation process must be transparent and clearly documented, as well as based on a sound scientific approach, if it is to be defensible.

An important task in risk evaluation is testing the sensitivity of the outcome of the assessment to changes in the assumptions used. This is particularly important in marginal cases where relatively small adjustments to the assumptions may have a significant effect on the risk estimate and major implications for the type and cost of any remedial action.

Risk control

It is important to define the level of residual contamination that equates to an acceptable level of risk. For the purposes of this guide, acceptable residual concentrations of contaminants in affected media following treatment are termed Contaminated Related Objectives or CROs. These play a major role in the selection, design and implementation of remedial action (see Chapters 4–7). It is essential that they are agreed in close consultation with the regulatory authorities, and other third parties (e.g. funders, insurers etc.) as appropriate. The choice of CROs will reflect site-specific factors.

CROs may chosen by:

— adopting generic assessment criteria (e.g. the ICRCL threshold trigger concentration value for cadmium in soil intended for residential use)
— adapting generic assessment criteria (in which site-specific factors have been used to adjust a generic value)
— deriving values from a site-specific risk assessment.

Selection of CROs is vital and should be the subject of careful consideration. While the ICRCL threshold trigger concentrations may be appropriate in certain circumstances, this will not always be the case. For example, in the evaluation of CROs for remedial treatment of an operational site the ICRCL values have no specific standing.

Additional indirect criteria may have to be set in order to ensure that CROs are met. For example, it may be necessary to specify the permeability of barrier materials used in an in-ground containment system that must be met in order to meet CROs for groundwater quality.

Reporting

Completion of site investigation and assessment often marks a natural break in the life of a contaminated land project, indicating the completion of a substantial part of the assessment process and the beginning of the remedial design phase. In practice it may also involve a change in personnel. Given the fundamental role of site investigation and assessment in the risk management process as a whole, and the fact that detailed knowledge about a site may be lost as a result of personnel changes, it is essential that a full and comprehensive account of all site investigation and assessment work and findings is prepared.

Site investigation and risk assessment reports should provide the following.

(a) A description of the decision-making framework including investigation objectives and any constraints, such as a lack of time, inadequate financial resources, practical difficulties (e.g. restricted access to parts of the site) that may have applied to any phase of investigation and risk assessment.

(b) A factual account of all the work carried out, supported as appropriate with graphical material in the form of maps, photographs, sampling and analytical procedures etc.

(c) The findings of the investigation including field observations, analytical results, monitoring data etc.

(d) The findings of the risk assessment, including the identity and status of any reference data used in the assessment, an analysis of uncertainties, and details of any assumptions, safety factors etc. used to complete the analysis.

(e) Recommended CROs and other technical objectives.

(f) An analysis of any technical or practical constraints that are likely to affect the type of remedial action that can be taken at the site.

Part II Remediation

4. Remedial action as part of risk management

Introduction

Risk reduction through remedial action is the final element in managing the risks associated with contaminated land (see Chapters 1–3). It comes into play when, on the basis of a risk assessment, it is decided that the site poses unacceptable risks to specified targets and action should be taken to reduce or control the risks to an acceptable level.

Typically, a number of remedial options will be available to the assessor, but only one (or one combination) will offer the best overall balance between technical effectiveness, practicality and cost.

The purpose of risk reduction is therefore to:
— specify acceptable levels of risk reduction/control
— identify a remedial strategy that will meet risk reduction/control, and other objectives
— design and implement the strategy
— ensure through a programme of monitoring and validation that remedial objectives have been met.

Remedy selection, design and implementation normally follow on from site investigation and assessment, and the identification of Contamination Related Objectives (CROs) (see Chapter 3). However, there is overlap between the various stages and there may be a need to carry out supplementary investigation or other studies before a detailed design can be finalised.

The following chapters are concerned principally with the use of technical measures for controlling/reducing the risks associated with contaminated land. However, it is possible to control risks using administrative means (see Box 4.1).

Administrative measures may be effective where hazards, pathways and targets are specifically related to the use of the land (e.g. direct access by children to contaminants at the surface, direct contact by service pipes to contaminants in the ground). They are not applicable where the contaminant is mobile, migrating off-site and, as a result, is threatening sensitive surface or groundwater bodies or other targets. The use of administrative measures alone also means that there is no material improvement in the condition of the land: the same situation will have to be confronted again in the future should the condition or use of the site change.

Box 4.1 Examples of administrative means of controlling the risks associated with contaminated land

- Adopting a 'less sensitive' use of the land (e.g. substituting commercial/industrial for residential/horticultural use: formal restrictions on the use of the land may have to be made)
- Restricting access to the site
- Altering the form or layout of a development (e.g. to avoid areas of severe contamination)

Note. It may be necessary to include control measures in site management documents (and to disclose these in the event of sale) where administrative means are used to control or reduce risks.

Remedy selection

Remedial methods selected for use must be:

— applicable to the contaminant and media (e.g. soil, sediment, construction debris, surface/groundwater etc.) to be treated
— effective in achieving specified Contamination Related Objectives
— feasible in the sense that they can be put into practical effect
— acceptable to all relevant parties
— economic.

In practice, each remedial method has advantages and limitations that may constrain its use on a site-specific basis. The purpose of remedy selection is to identify and then evaluate remedial methods (or combinations of methods) which may be suitable for use on a particular site, with the aim of identifying that remedial strategy (the preferred remedial strategy) best able to satisfy site-specific remedial objectives and overcome constraints.

Design and implementation

Design and implementation is that part of risk reduction which transforms a remedial strategy from a conceptual state into practical action at the site.

To a large extent, the same principles of design and implementation employed in conventional civil engineering/construction applications can be applied to the remediation of contaminated land: in some cases the same practical techniques can be employed.

However, the presence of hazardous substances on contaminated sites, and the relative lack of well established guidance in this field (e.g. Codes of Practice, standard contract terms and conditions, technical specifications etc.) means that conventional approaches and tools may not be directly applicable: in some cases (e.g. the application of a chemical or biological treatment process) they may be of very limited value. Other elements of remedial design and implementation, such as the use of treatability testing or pilot trials in the early stages of selection and design, are largely unfamiliar in a conventional civil engineering context and special provision may have to be made to incorporate these elements into the design and implementation process.

The process of design and implementation of a remedial strategy can involve a significant period of time and it is important to recognise this, particularly in the context of a redevelopment project where there may be pressures to reduce or minimise the scheme programme.

Key aspects of design and implementation in land remediation applications are listed in Box 4.2.

Box 4.2 Key aspects of design and implementation

Design	Implementation
Design	**Implementation**
• Identifying objectives and constraints	• Project supervision
• Planning, design and specification	• Communication
• Procurement options	• Monitoring and validation
• Contract options	• Post-treatment management (where appropriate)
	• Documentation and reporting

These aspects are important because they help to ensure not only that remedial action will achieve its objectives, but also that comprehensive evidence is collected to demonstrate that remedial objectives have been met.

5. Remedial options

Classification and terminology

There is no universally accepted classification of, or terminology for, remedial methods. For the purposes of this Guide the approach used in the CIRIA guidance document on the Remedial Treatment of Contaminated Land[2] has been adopted.

Currently available methods can be classified into two broad groups (see Figure 3):

(a) *Civil engineering based methods*: these employ conventional civil engineering techniques to remove or contain contamination sources, or to block the pathways by which contaminants reach targets.

(b) *Process-based methods*: these use specific physical, chemical and biological processes to remove, destroy, or modify contaminants.

The two groups are not mutually exclusive and there are remedial methods used under certain circumstances, such as the use of compaction techniques to reduce the likelihood of combustion of susceptible materials, which do not readily fall into either category. However, their classification provides a useful basis for considering remedial methods available for treating contaminated soils, sediments and water. A remedial strategy may incorporate methods from each group, or use a number of different methods on an integrated basis, to achieve specified remedial objectives. Other important terms that may be encountered in a remedial context are listed in Box 5.1.

Box 5.1 Important remedial terms

- *Ex-situ remediation*: where treatment is applied following the excavation (in the case of solids) or extraction (in the case of liquids and gases) of contaminated material
- *In-situ remediation*: where treatment is applied to contaminated media without prior removal from the ground
- *On-site and off-site remediation*: relate to the location of treatment. All in-situ treatment is carried out on the site undergoing remediation, but ex-situ treatment may be carried out on-site (for example using mobile treatment plant) or at centralised/merchant facilities off-site (e.g. hazardous waste incineration, physical-chemical waste treatment etc.)
- *Treatment*: used in its normal sense to imply some material improvement in the condition of a site. It is not intended as a comment on the quality or permanence of a particular method

Civil engineering based methods

Civil engineering based methods can be classified into three main groups:

(a) **removal** (excavation) of contaminated solid material.
(b) **physical containment** (of the contaminated ground) using covers and in-ground barriers.
(c) **hydraulic controls**, used in support of a and b above; as the principal means of control; or specifically for the treatment of contaminated surface or groundwater.

In general, civil engineering based methods are relatively insensitive to variations in the concentrations and types of contaminants present, or the types of contaminated media being handled. In this respect they are of potentially wide applicability. They are also well established, familiar to both designers and contractors, and use readily available plant and equipment. However, they suffer from a number of limitations: for example, excavation may pose health and environmental impacts; containment systems do not materially reduce the volume or the hazardous properties of contaminated material, they have a finite life and their effectiveness is thought to decrease over time.

More detailed information on the capabilities and limitations of individual civil engineering based methods of treatment are provided in Appendix C and reference 2.

Process-based methods

Process-based methods can be classified into five main generic types:

(a) **thermal treatment**: using heat to remove, stabilise or destroy contaminants
(b) **physical treatment**: using physical processes, or exploiting physical attributes, to separate contaminants from host media, or different fractions of contaminated media
(c) **chemical treatment**: using chemical reactions to remove, destroy or modify contaminants
(d) **biological treatment**: using natural metabolic pathways of micro-organisms and other biological agents to remove, destroy or modify contaminants
(e) **stabilisation/solidification**: in which contaminants are chemically stabilised and/or immobilised to reduce their availability to targets.

Compared to civil engineering methods, process-based methods of treatment have much more specific capabilities and requirements. As a result they tend to be restricted to a more limited range of contaminants and media. However, many have the advantage of reducing the volume or concentration of hazardous substances in affected media and, if they also destroy contaminants, may provide a more 'permanent' solution to the contamination.

Generic processes can be applied in either an ex-situ or in-situ mode. In-situ applications avoid the cost and potential above-ground environmental impacts associated with excavation/extraction. However, at the present time, there is generally less practical experience in the application of in-situ methods compared with their ex-situ counterparts. It may also be more difficult in practice to predict (or demonstrate) the outcome of an in-situ application, or to optimise/control the process once in operation.

More detailed information on the capabilities and limitations of individual process-based methods of treatment is provided in Appendix C and references 2 and 36–38.

Figure 3 Classification of remedial methods

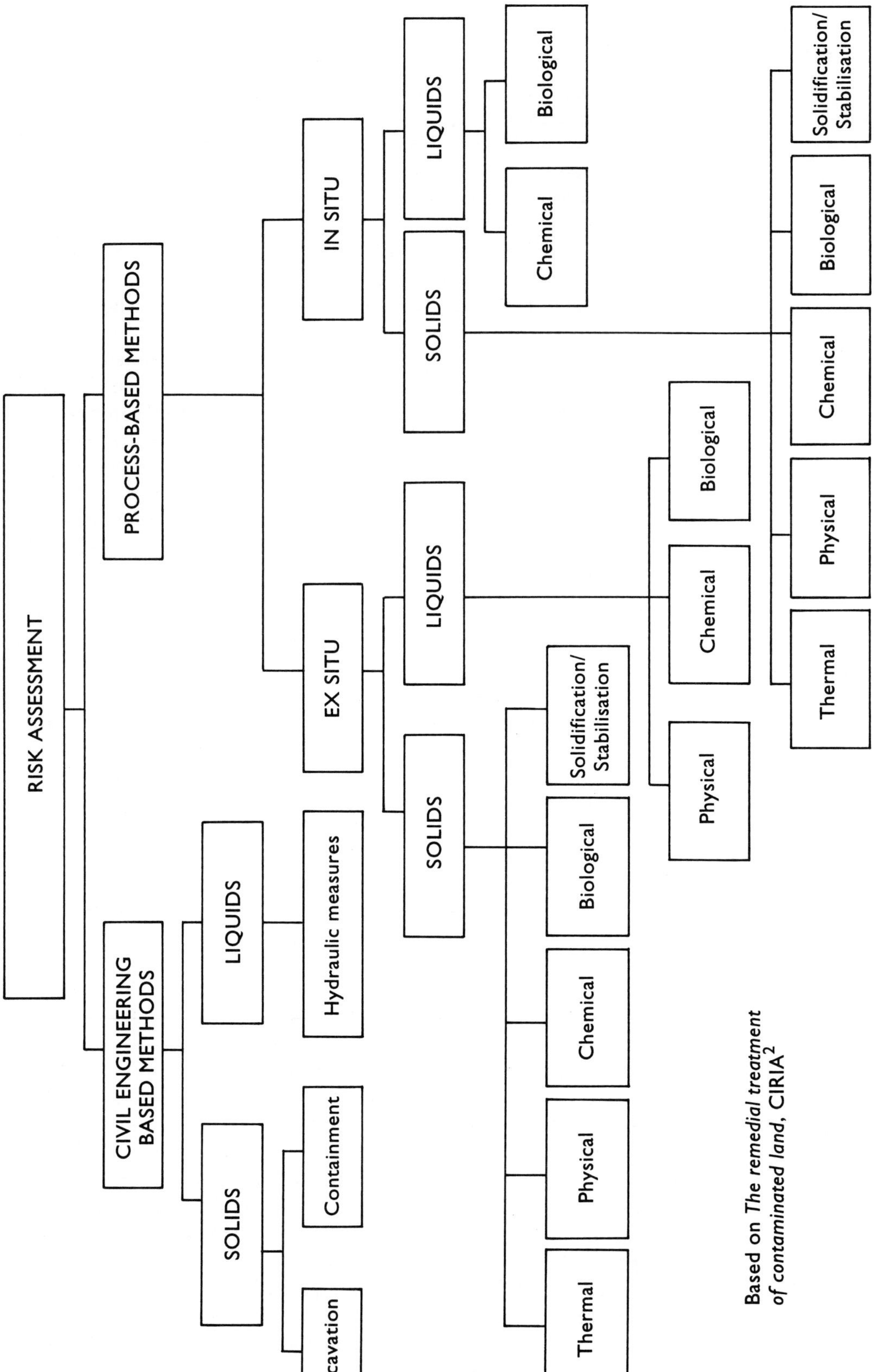

Based on *The remedial treatment of contaminated land*, CIRIA[2]

6. Remedy selection

The selection process

In some cases a strategy based on a single remedial method may be sufficient to address all of the risks presented by the site. Alternatively, a range of different methods may have to be combined to provide an integrated remedial strategy capable of dealing with different types of contaminants, or different parts of the site. Although CROs should have priority in determining the type of remedial action taken, it will usually be necessary to meet other technical objectives (e.g. on the engineering properties of the site) and overcome practical and cost constraints.[2] The main purpose of selection is therefore to:

(a) identify those remedial methods most likely to be applicable, effective and feasible on a site-area or media-specific basis,

(b) develop a range of potentially applicable, effective and feasible strategies based on a short-list of favourable methods and

(c) evaluate individual strategies (which might comprise one or a combination of specific methods) to determine which is most likely to offer the best balance between technical effectiveness, practicality and cost.

Selection is a staged process of identification, evaluation and screening (see Figure 4) by which some remedial methods (or strategies) are retained for further consideration and others are rejected. The use of selection criteria (see Selection criteria and procedures, below) can help to keep the process both manageable and objective.

A structured framework encourages thorough consideration of available options (and their practical and cost implications), and helps to avoid the development of inappropriate strategies based on too few data and an inadequate assessment of alternatives. It also helps the designer to anticipate the potential benefits and limitations of different types of approach that otherwise might not be readily apparent. By requiring the designer to present the rationale for acceptance/ rejection decisions, the selection process also makes decision-making more transparent and accessible to third parties. This is important when discussing a proposed course of action with the regulatory authorities and the local community, and in the future, when a remediated site is sold or its ownership transferred.

The scope of the selection process and the way in which decisions about remedial action are made in practice will vary to an extent depending on the exact circumstances of the site, the experience of the designer and the stage in the selection process. For example:

— preliminary views on potentially useful remedial methods may already have been formed during the detailed investigation and assessment of the site

Figure 4 The selection process

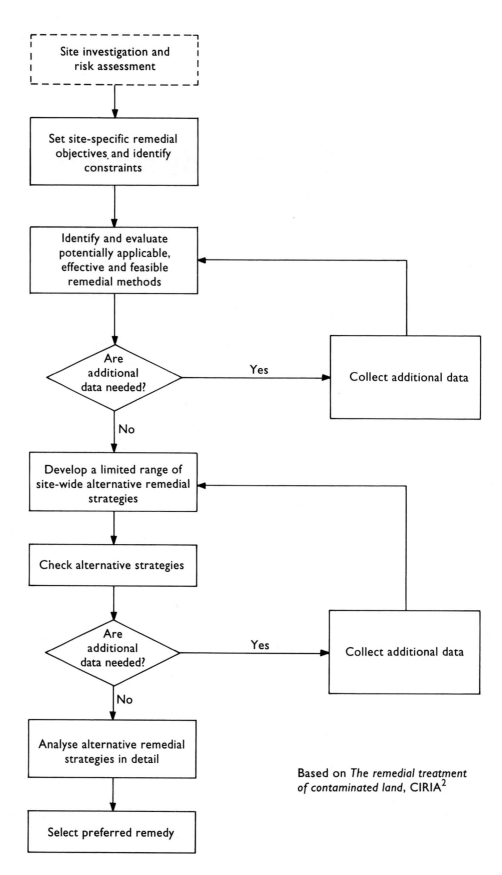

Based on *The remedial treatment of contaminated land*, CIRIA[2]

— it may be apparent at a very early stage that only a limited number of remedial options exist

— in some cases it may be necessary to review remedial objectives in the light of more information on site characteristics, and the capabilities and limitations of the various remedial methods.

Nevertheless, for the reasons outlined above, it is important to present a full justification of all acceptance/rejection decisions made during the selection process.

Initial selection decisions are typically made on the basis of experience, and published information readily available to the designer. Initial selection criteria (see below) can help in deciding which remedial methods are most likely to be suitable, given the specific circumstances of the site and its current or planned use. Selection of the preferred strategy should be based on a detailed analysis of a limited range of alternative remedial strategies. The use of final selection criteria and formal ranking systems may be beneficial during the detailed assessment stage. In some cases (particularly where process-based remedial methods are under consideration) it may be necessary to carry out bench or pilot-scale treatability studies (see Role of treatability studies, below) and/or supplementary site investigation to complete the detailed assessment.

Selection criteria and procedures

Initial selection and evaluation

Initially, remedial methods should be selected on the basis of their:

— applicability (to contaminants and media)
— likely effectiveness (in meeting CROs and other technical objectives)
— feasibility.

Selection criteria (see Box 6.1) can be used to help in the initial screening and evaluation of methods. Further information on initial selection criteria and their role in the selection process is summarised in Appendix E (see also reference 2).

Box 6.1 Initial selection criteria

• Applicability	• Time constraints
• Effectiveness	• Planning and management needs
• Limitations	• Health and safety needs
• Cost	• Potential for integration
• Development status/track record	• Environmental impacts
• Availability	• Monitoring
• Operational requirements	• Validation
• Information requirements	• Post-treatment management

The output from the first stage of selection should be a short-list of potentially viable remedial methods classified according to the media/zones of the site to be treated, approximate volumes of material involved, and CROs to be met.

Development of remedial strategies

Once a range of remedial methods for treating particular contaminants or parts of the site has been identified, those methods should be combined to develop a range of strategies for treating the site as a whole. A number of alternatives should be developed in the first instance so that there is some scope for choice during final selection when the technical sufficiency, feasibility and costs of alternative schemes are evaluated in detail. Unless the circumstances of the site dictate otherwise, a range of alternative strategies, from minimal action (perhaps at the expense of long-term security or limitations on the use of the site) to comprehensive action (perhaps at high initial costs) should be developed.

Combining remedial methods for operation on an integrated basis may have technical and practical implications. Checks should be made to ensure that remedial strategies are likely to remain applicable, effective and practical.

This stage of the evaluation also provides an opportunity to check:

— that CROs and other technical objectives remain valid and likely to be achievable in practice
— whether more detailed information, for example on site conditions or the anticipated performance of remedial methods, is needed in order to complete the assessment.

In the first instance, further desk-based research should be carried out to resolve any information gaps. It is important to bear in mind, however, that different remedial methods have quite specific information requirements and it may be necessary at this stage to carry out additional (i.e. supplementary) site investigation, or treatability studies, to provide the required data.

The output from this stage of selection should be a limited number of potentially applicable, effective and feasible remedial strategies which can then be taken forward for detailed evaluation.

Selection of the preferred remedy

In this stage of selection, alternative remedial strategies are analysed in detail to determine their respective strengths and weaknesses. Final selection criteria, addressing both long- and short-term objectives and operational issues (see Box 6.2), and formal ranking systems (see Table 6.1) may help in the assessment process.

Box 6.2 Examples of final selection criteria

Long-term criteria	**Short-term criteria**
• Legal compliance	• Acceptable operational requirements
• Long-term effectiveness	• Minimal short-term health and safety implications
• Acceptable track record of use	• Minimal short-term environmental impacts
• Reduction in toxicity, mobility and volume	
• Acceptability to local community	

Table 6.1 Example of formal ranking procedure for alternative remedial strategies

Criterion	Rank*	Weighting for each strategy§			Overall score for each strategy		
		A	B	C	A	B	C
Legal compliance	10	3	3	2	30	30	20
Long-term effectiveness	8	3	2	1	24	16	8
Reduction in hazard	6	3	2	1	18	12	6
Track record	4	3	3	3	12	12	12
Acceptability to local community	2	2	3	1	4	6	2
Operational require-ments	2	1	2	3	2	4	6
Short-term health and safety impacts	2	1	2	3	2	4	6
Short-term environ-mental impacts	2	2	2	1	4	4	2
Overall score					96	88	62

Note. Values in table are for illustrative purposes only.
* Ranks and weighting factors should reflect site-specific priorities.
§ High weighting reflects favourable attributes (e.g. good long-term effectiveness, insignificant operational requirements etc.)

The outcome of ranking, together with information on costs and the ability of each strategy to meet overall technical and administrative objectives, can then be used as a basis for selecting the preferred remedial strategy.

Role of treatability studies

Treatability studies are carried out to:

— provide site-specific information on the likely technical performance of a particular, process-based remedial method or strategy
— reduce technical and financial uncertainties associated with particular remedial strategies.

The need for treatability data may be identified during the initial screening of methods, or during the final assessment of alternative strategies. Because of the costs involved, treatability testing on any significant scale is only likely to be feasible when the designer is sure that a particular method has a reasonably good chance of being applied (i.e. once a method has reached the final assessment stage). However, it is important to note that the absence of treatability data at an early stage can result in an inappropriate method progressing a long way down the selection pathway before being eliminated. Since the need for treatability studies introduces a further stage into the process of remedial strategy selection and implementation, more time is required before the remediation work can be completed. Treatability studies can sometimes take a significant period of time and this may itself become a factor in the selection process.

Treatability tests should always be carried out where a method does not have a documented track record of use in the field, or where insufficient data are available to predict the likely outcome of treatment even where the contaminated matrix has been well defined.

Tests can be conducted at either bench or pilot-scale. It is important to document fully both the test plan (e.g. aims, methods, means of interpretation etc.) and the outcome (results, interpretation, conclusions, recommendations etc.). Issues to be addressed when developing a treatability test plan are summarised in Box 6.3. Further information on the design and application of treatability studies for the remediation of contaminated land is given in references 2 and 39.

Box 6.3 Issues to be addressed when developing treatability test plans

• Background information and rationale	• QA/QC plan
• Site characteristics	• Data management
• Properties of test material	• Data analysis and interpretation
• Test objectives	• Health and safety
• Procedures, equipment and materials	• Waste management
• Analytical methods	• Contingency planning

Note. Parameters apply to bench and pilot-scale testing: additional requirements for pilot scale work are:
— pilot plant installation and start-up
— plant operation and maintenance
— operating conditions to be tested
— sampling plan (for operational trials)

7. Design and implementation

Introduction

Design and implementation transform the preferred remedial strategy from its conceptual state into practical action in the field.

Site investigation, assessment and remedy selection should have been sufficient to:

— establish the overall goal of remedial action (i.e. to reduce/control the risks associated with contaminated land to acceptable levels)
— identify specific objectives (e.g. CROs, other technical objectives) for remedial action
— provide some idea (outline design) of the works needed to achieve stated objectives.

The next stage is to develop these outline requirements into a more detailed set of objectives and plans that can be used to implement the remedial strategy and demonstrate that remedial objectives have been met.

Planning and design

Project planning

The main purpose of project planning is to establish:

— what activities should take place to achieve the objectives of the project
— the relationship between the activities
— what resources (including time) should be made available to enable the activities to take place.

The advantages of project planning are that it:

— creates a more accurate picture of what should happen as a project progresses
— allows better anticipation of what needs to happen next
— allows critical points in a project to be identified
— permits more reliable estimates of resource requirements to be made
— allows better anticipation of, and planning for, bottlenecks in a project
— enhances co-operation and communication
— helps to build commitment between project participants
— assists in completion of the project according to the required standards, on time and within budget.

The results can be usefully presented in pictorial form, for example as bar or Gantt charts, or critical path charts.

It is essential that sufficient time and resources are made available for project planning and that it addresses both the management and technical aspects of the remedial project.

Technical design and specification

The technical output of project planning is the detailed design and specification. Clearly, these will vary depending on the circumstances of the site, the type of remedial action being proposed and the management objectives (e.g. timescales, costs, procurement preferences etc.) agreed for the project. Many of the technical aspects should have been addressed during investigation, assessment and remedy selection. The detailed technical design should therefore build on the information already assembled, taking care to address the main aspects listed in Box 7.1.

Box 7.1 Aspects to be addressed when developing the detailed technical design

- *CROs* (e.g. by site area, contaminant type)
- *Other technical objectives* (e.g. engineering properties)
- *Proposed remedial methods* (procedures, equipment, supply services, layout, phasing, materials handling and waste disposal)
- *Legal approvals and conditions* (see Management objectives and plan, below)
- *Duration, phasing and integration* (within remedial strategy itself and externally, e.g. with construction, landscaping etc.)
- *Environmental and public health protection measures* (e.g. containment measures, site security, habitat protection, noise, vehicle access and movements)
- *Occupational hygiene* (equipment and procedures)
- *Site preparation* (e.g. access, security, site services, site storage, laboratory support, decontamination facilities etc.)
- *Monitoring requirements* (for legal compliance, for process control and optimisation, for demonstrating long-term performance)
- *Validation requirements* (e.g. post-processing sampling and analysis, quality of excavated area, quality of materials used in remedial work)
- *Public relations* (e.g. information needs and procedures, contact points etc.)
- *Post-treatment management* (e.g. monitoring, administrative controls)

The technical specification should describe the scope of the proposed remedial work and the standards (e.g. of remediation, workmanship, materials etc.) to be achieved. It may be used to obtain contracting services through formal processes of tendering or negotiation.

Standard specifications may be available, or applicable with some adjustments, for some types of engineering based remedial strategies. In other cases the specification may have to be developed from first principles (see Procurement, below).

Management objectives and plan

Successful remediation depends as much on effective management as on technical objectives and performance. Experience shows that if the technical aspects and timing of a project are properly managed then costs are usually controlled as a result: moreover the earlier the discipline of control is introduced, the easier it is to manage subsequent phases of a project.[2] Two ways of ensuring appropriate technical and management control of a remedial project are:

— appointment of a project manager with specific responsibilities for managing the project, and
— development of a management plan.

The management plan is a statement describing the way in which it is proposed to organise and control remedial action. Its purpose is to assist in the development of the detailed design, making procurement and contract decisions and ensuring satisfactory overall control during implementation. Issues to be addressed during management planning are listed in Box 7.2.

Box 7.2 Issues to be addressed during management planning

> - The overall objectives (e.g. technical, financial, timescale, budget) of remedial action
> - Legal aspects and their impact on remedial action
> - The roles and responsibilities of the various participants
> - The preparation of a clear description (e.g. contract documents, specification, supporting information) of the strategy to be followed
> - The resources (e.g. financial, technical, personnel) required
> - Means of internal (e.g. between project participants) and external (e.g. with regulators and local community) communication
> - Health and safety issues (e.g. preparation of COSHH statement)
> - Risk of unexpected developments or emergencies, and how these should be handled
> - Supervision requirements
> - Agreement on the standards and procedures for checking progress and quality of the works, and demonstrating compliance with external requirements
> - Documentation systems to record all objectives, plans, decisions made and action taken, including modifications to the original design concept

The key technical and management aspects of project planning are:

(a) legal aspects
(b) team building
(c) resource planning
(d) contingency planning
(e) health and safety
(f) public health and environmental protection
(g) quality assurance and control
(h) monitoring, validation and post-treatment management.

Legal aspects

Land remediation projects may be subject to a wide range of legal provisions relating to land use planning and development control, public and occupational health, and environmental protection. Issues relevant to project planning include:

— whether and what type(s) of approval is required
— time and resource implications of obtaining approvals
— duration of approvals and implications of conditional approval for planned work

— implications for project specification and contractual arrangements
— implications for long-term post-remediation management.

Legislation governing waste management may also impact on remediation projects in various ways such as:

— temporary stockpiling of contaminated material before treatment or disposal off-site
— permanent containment systems
— handling and disposal of waste

In addition to the need to ensure compliance with the *Environmental Protection Act 1990* Duty of Care on waste, at all stages of the investigation and remediation process, there may also be a requirement for a waste management licence for either temporary or permanent storage of contaminated material on the site. This raises a number of issues, including that of surrender of the licence on completion of the works, the conditions for which have been made more stringent by the *Environmental Protection Act 1990* and the *Waste Management Licensing Regulations 1994*. The process of obtaining a licence may also add significantly to the project programme if the need for this is not established sufficiently early.

Table 7.1 gives brief guidance on the legal requirements which may apply to individual sites. It is important to note that the guidance refers to the position in England and Wales (different arrangements may apply in Scotland and Northern Ireland — see reference 2 for further details) and that the legal framework changes from time to time. Detailed requirements will vary depending on the exact circumstances of the site: specialist legal advice may be required in relation to individual projects. Further information on the regulatory framework for contaminated land in the UK can be found in reference 2.

In addition to those legal provisions listed in Table 7.1, the *Environmental Protection Act 1990, section 143* also provides for the preparation by local authorities of Public Registers of Land which may be contaminated. Department of the Environment proposals for regulations to implement this were withdrawn, however, in March 1993 and a wide-ranging review initiated by Government.

Team building

This is essential to ensure that:

— the right level of experience and combination of skills are available for remediation
— key roles and responsibilities are assigned to appropriately qualified and experienced organisations and individuals
— there is effective communication and co-operation between project participants
— there is agreement (on project objectives) and commitment (without which the project is unlikely to achieve its objectives) between project participants.

The composition of the team will depend on procurement decisions, although team building is likely to be one of the first tasks assigned to a project manager. The importance of a multi-disciplinary approach to contaminated land projects should not be overlooked when formulating the team. Site supervision plays a critical role in ensuring that remedial objectives are met (see Implementation, below) and it is important to ensure that only appropriately qualified individuals are assigned to this task.

Table 7.1 Legal provisions which may apply to remedial action

Area of law	Legal provision	Requirement
Land use planning and development control	Town and Country Planning legislation	Permission for development (which may include engineering or remedial works in some circumstances)
	Building Act and Building Regulations	Duties to ensure the safety of buildings and those affected by buildings
Public health	Environmental Protection Act 1990	Obligation to prevent the creation of a statutory nuisance (e.g. generation of toxic vapours, dusts etc.)
	Occupier Liability legislation	Obligation to ensure the safety of visitors (which may include trespassers) to premises
Health and safety	Health and Safety at Work etc. Act, 1974 and associated regulations	Obligation to protect the health and safety of employees and the general public from hazards arising at a place of work
Environmental protection:		
Air	Control of Pollution Act 1974	Powers to local authorities to make enquiries about air pollution from any premises, except private dwellings
Water	Water Resources Act 1991	Prior authorisation required from National Rivers Authority (NRA) to make a discharge of polluting substances to controlled waters
		Prior authorisation required for the abstraction of water (e.g. to control groundwater levels, during the installation of in-ground barriers, during groundwater remediation operations) in some circumstances
		Powers to NRA to protect the aqueous environment and to remedy or forestall pollution of controlled waters
	Water Industry Act 1991	Prior authorisation required from the sewerage undertaker to make a discharge of polluting material to a sewer

Table 7.1 Legal provisions which may apply to remedial action – continued

Area of law	Legal provision	Requirement
Waste	Environmental Protection Act 1990 and associated regulations	Duty of Care on all those involved in the production, handling and disposal of controlled waste (e.g. contaminated excavation arisings) to ensure that they follow safe, authorised, and properly documented procedures and practices
		Provides for the definition of controlled waste and arrangements for licensing waste management facilities and operations. For on-site disposal these may include requirements for management of the facility by 'fit and proper persons' with appropriate 'certificates of technical competence'. Post-closure monitoring and 'certificates of closure' will normally also be required. Specific regulations cover registration of carriers of waste and waste brokers, and matters related to Special Waste
		Provides for the authorisation (under Her Majesty's Inspectorate of Pollution or local authority control) for the operation of prescribed processes
		Provides for the authorisation of mobile treatment plant
Protected areas, species and artifacts	Town and Country Planning Act, 1990; Wildlife and Countryside Act, 1981; Ancient Monuments and Archaeological Areas Act, 1979	Protection of designated areas (e.g. Sites of Special Scientific Interest), species (e.g. plants and animals) and artifacts (e.g. ancient monuments)

Resource planning

Resource planning is closely related to the detailed design (see Technical design and specification, above) and is therefore highly dependent on the type of remedial action being proposed. Resource planning should address three main aspects:

(a) personnel requirements (see above and Procurement, below)
(b) materials, for example in relation to:

— types (e.g. cover and barrier materials, replacement materials; treatment chemicals and agents; fuel; water etc.)
— amounts (in total, over time)
— sources (e.g. availability, reliability of supply, costs)
— means of transport and storage

(c) equipment, for example in relation to:

— types (e.g. excavation plant, process plant, transport vehicles, health and safety equipment)
— quantity (in total, at particular times)
— sources
— site access
— operational requirements (e.g. site, services, laboratory support, monitoring equipment)
— repair and maintenance arrangements.

Resource requirements may change radically over the remedial period, particularly where an integrated approach has been adopted. It is also important to ensure that resource planning addresses essential ancillary activities, such as monitoring, validation, environmental protection etc., as well as the main programme of remedial work.

Contingency planning

Although thorough planning should minimise the risk of disruption or delay to remedial operations, in land remediation projects there is usually some scope for unexpected or emergency situations to arise. Contingency planning is a means of identifying, analysing and planning for unexpected events so that if they do occur, they can be addressed with minimal impact on the rest of the planned operations. Contingency planning involves:

— identifying the types of unwanted event that may arise
— assessing the likelihood that an unwanted event will occur
— developing contingency arrangements to deal with problems that do occur.

Examples of the types of event that may warrant contingency planning during remedial action are listed in Box 7.3.

Box 7.3 Examples of unwanted events during remedial projects

- Encountering larger than expected or unexpected areas or types of contamination
- Accidents and emergencies (e.g. fire, explosion, collapse of unstable ground during excavation)
- Failure of remedial system to achieve specified objectives
- Failure of a component or supply of materials
- Adverse weather conditions
- Regulatory intervention due to failure to achieve compliance with specified conditions

Health and safety

Ensuring the protection of site workers is an important aspect of planning the remedial strategy. Site workers may be exposed to health risks through:

— exposure to contaminated site materials
— exposure to other hazardous substances (e.g. chemical treatment agents) used during the remedial operations themselves
— operation of hazardous equipment and plant (e.g. heavy excavation plant, transport vehicles, process plant operated at high temperatures or pressures)
— hazardous by-products or wastes in gaseous, liquid or solid form.

Health and safety provision should reflect site-specific requirements. Aspects to be addressed at the planning stage include those listed in Box 7.4. There will normally be a requirement to undertake a COSHH assessment prior to any remedial works. For this, and to assist with the contractor's overall under-standing of the contamination conditions and hence health and safety risks, all available data on the chemical regime and site conditions generally should be provided to the contractor before work begins.

Box 7.4 Health and safety aspects to be addressed during remedial action

Health and safety procedures	**Health and safety equipment**
• Controlled entry (permit to work) procedures (where applicable)	• Washing and eating facilities
• Site zoning (i.e. 'dirty' and clean areas)	• Protective clothing (e.g. for eyes, head, hands and feet)
• Good hygiene (e.g. no smoking, eating except in designated areas)	• Monitoring equipment (e.g. personal exposure, ambient concentrations)
• Monitoring (e.g. for on-, off-site-toxic/hazardous gases)	• Respiratory equipment
• Appropriate disposal of wastes	• First aid box
• Safe handling, storage and trans-port of hazardous samples	• Telephone link
• Control of nuisance (e.g. noise, vibration, dust and odour)	• Decontamination facilities (e.g. for boots, clothing, machinery)
• Emergency procedures	
• Provision of appropriate training (e.g. to recognise hazards, use equipment)	
• Need for routine health surveil-lance	
• Notification to hospital, Health and Safety Executive, Environ-mental Health Officer	

More detailed guidance on the health and safety implications of contaminated land can be found in references 3 and 17. Guidance on the potential health and safety impacts of particular remedial methods can be found in references 2 and 37.

Public health and environmental protection

Remedial action may pose significant short-term public health and/or environ-mental impacts through, for example:

— emission of hazardous gases, liquids or solids, including dust and odour
— generation of noise, heat, vibration.

The type and severity of potential public health and environmental impacts, and the control measures taken to reduce them (e.g. containment/treatment of hazardous emissions, location and hours of operation of heavy plant) will vary depending on the type of remedial action being proposed and site-specific factors (e.g. presence of residential areas, sensitive surface waters etc). However, there may be a legal obligation both to implement control measures and to demon-strate through monitoring that they are effective (see below).

Quality assurance and control

Quality assurance/quality control (QA/QC) procedures can aid the proper management and control of remedial projects by:

— encouraging the systematic planning, organisation, control and documentation of a remedial project
— improving the attitude of both purchasers (the client) and suppliers (e.g. consultants, contractors and sub-contractors) to contractual obligations
— minimising the risks of misunderstandings and disputes
— increasing the prospect of achieving the required end-point.

Quality management procedures, such as those set out in BS 5750,[18] can be applied to site-specific remedial operations provided that account is taken of the essentially 'one-off' nature of such projects.

In principle, QA/QC provisions could be applied to the full range of activities carried out during the remediation of contaminated land including, for example:

— preparation of technical specifications and management plans
— procurement
— preparation of contract and supporting documents
— health and safety
— public health and environmental protection
— supervision, monitoring and validation of remedial work
— post-treatment management.

The CROs and other objectives set for the remedial work will provide the base data for QA/QC systems, particularly in relation to technical specification and validation work.

In practice, care is required in invoking QA/QC provisions as contractual obligations because they may introduce a duty of care where none previously existed, or conflict with requirements specified elsewhere in the contract.[40] More detailed information and guidance on the application of QA/QC to contaminated land projects can be found in reference 2 and, to civil engineering projects in general, in reference 41.

Monitoring, validation and post-treatment management

Monitoring, validation and post-treatment management are the principal means by which the performance of remedial action is measured and documented (see Implementation, below). It is essential that all associated requirements are fully addressed at the detailed planning stage, and that specific provision is made for them in contract documents.

Procurement

Project organisation

Procurement is the process of obtaining the goods and services needed to carry out the proposed remedial works. Procurement is guided by decisions made during management planning on the proposed organisation of the project, the various roles and responsibilities involved, and how these should be allocated.

Typically there are three main participants in land remediation projects:

(*a*) the client
(*b*) the client's professional advisors
(*c*) contractors and sub-contractors.

The identity of the participants varies depending on the exact circumstances of the site and the type of remedial action under consideration. Examples of possible participants in a land remediation project are listed in Box 7.5. It is important to recognise the multi-disciplinary nature of contaminated land projects. In order to allow access to the appropriate levels and types of expertise, it is usually necessary to employ more than one advisor and more than one contractor on such projects. The benefits of specialist input to both the professional team and the contracting organisations can be very significant to all involved in the project and should not be overlooked.

Box 7.5 Possible participants in a land remediation project

Client	**Advisors**	**Contractors/sub-contractors**
• Site owner (e.g. manufacturing industry, local authority, Development Corporation) • Liquidator/receiver • Regulatory authority (e.g. National Rivers Authority)	• Environmental consultant • Engineering consultant • Chemical engineering consultant • Financial consultant • Project management consultant	• Civil engineering contractor • Specialist land remediation contractor • Waste disposal contractor • Analytical laboratory • Land surveyors • Plant hire and machinery contractor • Construction materials supplier

In addition to the main participants, there may be a number of other parties with an interest in, or responsibility for, different aspects of remedial action, including:

— the regulatory authorities (e.g. local planning and environmental health departments, building inspectors, waste regulation authority, Health and Safety Executive)
— insurers and funders
— the local community
— special interest groups (e.g. natural history, heritage and archaeological protection groups).

It is the responsibility of the main participants to ensure that the interests of these other groups are fully addressed during the planning and implementation of remedial action.

Approaches to procurement

The procurement decisions of the client will depend on:

— nature, size, complexity and duration of remedial action
— resources and skills available to the client
— personal preferences of the client.

In practice, there are two main options as follows.

(a) **Conventional approach** where the services of a contractor are procured against a specification developed by the client (or more usually by an independent design organisation acting for the client). The specification may be:

— **method-based** in which the full scope of the required works and the procedures to be used are specified in detail: in this case the contractor is responsible for ensuring that the works conform to the specification

— **performance-based** in which the required end-points are specified by the designer but the contractor is permitted to submit proposals for the methods and materials to be used to achieve the required outcome. Once these have been approved by the client, the contractor is responsible for ensuring that the specified performance is achieved, agreed procedures are followed and approved materials are used. In this instance, the specified performance requirements may be compliance with the CROs.

(b) **Design and implement** in which a single organisation (a design and implement contractor) is responsible for both the design and contracting elements of the work.

The two approaches have different benefits and limitations in conventional civil engineering and construction projects:[42] potential advantages and disadvantages in a contaminated land context are listed in Table 7.2.

Table 7.2 Potential advantages and limitations of different approaches to procurement

	Conventional approach	**Design and implement**
Potential advantages	Independence of design	Only one organisation involved, therefore simplified administration and allocation of responsibility
	Full range of remedial options can be considered	
	Allows time for development of strategy before commitment is made to contractor	Contractor's experience of effective working methods can be taken into account in design
	Competitive tender on basis of a single design	Project duration can be reduced if design and contracting elements overlap
	Scope for small design changes at early stage without significant effect on costs	Firm price for work at early stage
	Allows for major design changes but only at significant cost and time penalties	

*Table 7.2 Potential advantages and limitations of different approaches to procurement —
continued*

	Conventional approach	**Design and implement**
Potential limitations	Administrative aspects more complex and responsibilities may be blurred	Availability of suitable contractor may be more limited
	Design does not benefit from contractor input	May reduce independence of design and scope for consideration of remedial options
	Project duration may be longer because no overlap of design and contracting elements	Limited scope for redressing poor performance by strengthening input of other project participants
	Badly handled design changes can increase costs and lead to delay	May increase time pressures and reduce scope for phasing

In the UK, experience in the use of a design and implement approach to remediation is still relatively limited and it is perhaps too early to judge what the actual benefits and limitations might be. However, whatever procurement route is adopted it is essential to ensure that:

— sufficient time and resources are available to complete the remedial design
— assessment and remedy selection are fully independent of potential contractor bias (in the case of design and implement, this can be achieved by providing independent review of submitted proposals)
— some form of warranty (or independent verification) is provided to ensure that remedial objectives have been met.

Contracts

The formation of a contract between the project participants marks an important stage, indicating certainty about the best way of organising and controlling a project, and a commitment on the part of the client to proceed.

All contracts should:

— establish initial requirements and obligations
— describe the procedures to be used by the client to order changes to planned work, and the means of compensating the contractor for breaches of the contract by the client
— specify procedures for access, inspection, correction of defects and enforcement.

Standard forms of contract are available. In practice, only conventional admeasurement (e.g. using the ICE Conditions of Contract[43] and Civil Engineering Standard Method of Measurement[44]) and design/build forms of contract (e.g. ICE[45]) have been employed to any great extent, although others such as those produced by the Institution of Chemical Engineers[46] have been used on some projects.

The standard forms of contract and technical specifications used in conventional civil engineering applications may have to be modified considerably so that they can applied in a remedial context. Where remediation involves the use of process-based methods of treatment, both technical specifications and contract terms may have to be developed from first principles. Modifying standard specifications and contract forms, or developing them for the first time, is a specialist activity and it is essential that this is done only by appropriately qualified staff.

Given the inherent uncertainties typically associated with contaminated land, and despite the legal authority of contracts, experience shows that defects in the outcome of remedial action are common, and significant resources may be wasted in disputing claims. The use of quality management systems has been suggested as one means of avoiding or minimising errors, and improving the quality of the finished product (see Quality assurance and control, above). Another possible approach is risk-sharing in which all participants (the client, professional advisors and contractors) accept the existence of uncertainty at the outset and undertake to share the commercial risks associated with the project on an equitable basis. However, risk-sharing in the context of land remediation is a relatively new concept: as yet there is little published information or practical experience on this type of contractual approach.

Selection of organisations

The remediation of contaminated land is a specialist and multi-disciplinary activity and it is essential that procurement delivers the right mix (of disciplines and skills) and experience to the project. Requirements will be site-specific but the factors listed in Box 7.6 should be addressed when considering the selection of potential consultants and contractors.

Box 7.6 Factors to be addressed when procuring assistance to a project

- Qualifications and experience of staff
- Track record (of individuals and organisations)
- Ability to provide named staff
- Understanding of policy, legal and technical basis of the work
- Familiarity with and use of relevant guidance (e.g. Codes of Practice, policy documents, technical guidance)
- Use of quality management systems
- Satisfactory performance in previous commissions
- Ability to provide applicable insurance cover (e.g. Professional Indemnity Insurance), warranties or other guarantees commensurate with the value and risks of the project

Implementation

Project supervision

It is essential to ensure a high standard of supervision if remedial projects are to achieve their objectives. Under conventional procurement and contract arrangements good supervision is essential for:

— monitoring quality and progress
— anticipating and dealing with unexpected developments
— initiating, agreeing, documenting and controlling changes to a planned programme of work
— accepting completed work

— identifying non-conforming work and ensuring that corrective action is taken

— ensuring that the reporting and documentation requirements of the project are met.

Although the supervisory role of the client is different under design and implement arrangements, it is essential that the client maintains an effective presence on site throughout the remedial period.

The importance of good supervision cannot be over-stressed. Failure to provide appropriately qualified and experienced supervision may mean that specified objectives are not met, and could lead to uncertainty about the safety and effectiveness of remedial action, time delays and cost overruns. It also jeopardises all the resources put into the project to get it to the stage of implementation. In a broader context, it may reduce the commercial value of a remediated site.

Communication

In conventional civil engineering and construction projects a lack of clear and effective communication between participants is a common cause of defects in the completed work.[42] The potential for error is much greater in contaminated land projects because:

— the information being transmitted may be complex and subject to uncertainty

— the relative lack of codified forms of information or instruction for land remediation projects can make the process of communication more cumbersome and more prone to errors.

Appropriate provision for internal communications (e.g. giving and receiving instructions, agreeing variations, reporting progress etc.) should be made in management plans and contracts. Special care is needed in the development of communication procedures for third parties, especially the local community where specialist technical expertise is generally not available. Examples of measures that may be considered appropriate for local community purposes are listed in Box 7.7.

Box 7.7 Examples of communication measures for local community

- Providing clear and user-friendly information on objectives, scope, duration, and expected outcome of remedial action
- Encouraging establishment of local liaison committee
- Providing regular opportunities and venues for liaison
- Providing a point of contact for times outside regular liaison sessions
- Arranging periodic site visits
- Preparing progress reports (e.g. on main site works, ancillary works such as boundary air quality monitoring)
- Establishing a complaints procedure and means of response

Monitoring and validation

Monitoring and validation are essential elements of project implementation because they provide a means of controlling the technical content of the work and demonstrating that remedial objectives have been met. Depending on the type of remedial action taken, monitoring may be carried out:

— to optimise and control a remedial operation
— to demonstrate compliance with legal requirements (e.g. discharge of an effluent to sewer)
— in support of public health and environmental protection (e.g. boundary air quality monitoring, surface water quality monitoring).

Validation is a particular form of monitoring carried out on an essentially 'one-off' basis. Its purpose is to confirm that remedial objectives have been met in relation to the whole, or parts, of a site. The status of validation data is significantly different to that of routine monitoring data because the acceptance of validation data by the supervising organisation can signify agreement that the contractual obligations of the work have been met. Validation arrangements may therefore have significant implications for the professional indemnity and/or warranties offered by the supervising organisation.

Monitoring and validation requirements should be made explicit in project plans (management plans and detailed design) and in contract documents. Issues to be addressed when developing monitoring and validation plans are listed in Box 7.8.

Box 7.8 Issues to be addressed when developing monitoring and validation plans

- Objectives
- Responsibilities
- Procedures (numbers, frequency and location of monitoring/validation points and methods of analysis etc.)
- QA/QC
- Interpretation
- Record keeping and reporting
- Response to monitoring/validation results

Monitoring and validation may be subject to regulatory control (e.g. through conditions attached to a planning permission or obligation, discharge consent, operating authorisation or waste management licence). In all cases it is essential to secure agreement on terms, including the degree of tolerance (if any) attached to monitoring/validation results, methodology to be used and the action to be taken in the event of non-compliance with agreed limits.

Post-treatment management

Where remedial action does not remove or destroy contaminants, or where there is uncertainty about its precise end-point (for example in some in-situ or groundwater remediation applications) there may be a need to provide for long-term management and aftercare. Post-treatment management obligations may be imposed by the regulatory authorities.

Post-treatment management may involve:

— on-going technical monitoring to establish the effectiveness of remedial action over the long-term (e.g. where an in-ground barrier has been installed, or some form of in-situ treatment has been applied)

— administrative controls (for example restrictions on certain types of construction/maintenance operations in the future where a surface cover has been installed).

It is important to address the practical, commercial and contractual implications at an early stage in planning a remedial project. Aspects to be addressed include:

— the nature, scope and duration of post-treatment management obligations
— responsibilities
— record keeping and reporting requirements.

Documentation and reporting

Project meetings and records provide the most reliable means of presenting and retaining information about remedial projects, including the detailed design and implementation stage. It is essential that project records cover any departures from the original design concept and associated work programmes.

Record keeping and reporting should extend to progress meetings and reports, as well as project completion.

For reasons of commercial confidence in the effectiveness and safety of a remediated site, it is essential that accurate records are kept of all remedial work done, including the results of validation and monitoring programmes, details of any regulatory involvement or requirements, and any administrative controls that may affect the long-term use of the site or security of installed measures.

A Final Completion Report should be prepared for each project, addressing the items listed in Box 7.9. Maintenance manuals will be needed for those projects where the remedial works require long-term monitoring and maintenance.

Box 7.9 Typical content of a Final Completion Report

- Decommissioning, decontamination and demolition record (where appropriate)
- Site investigation and risk assessment
- Selection of remedial methods and outline design
- Detailed design and procurement
- Progress reports and meetings
- Current status including post-treatment management requirements (where appropriate)
- Technical appendices

Appendix A Summary of information sources for desk study

Sources of information for desk study

General sources

Site records (e.g. drawings, production logs, environmental audits)

Company records (e.g. archival information, title deeds)

Maps (e.g. O.S., town maps, geological maps)

Photographic material (e.g. aerial photographs)

Directories (e.g. trade directories)

Local literature (e.g. local newspapers, local societies)

Site personnel (e.g. plant manager, safety officer)

Regulatory authorities (e.g. local council, National Rivers Authority, Her Majesty's Inspectorate of Pollution, Health and Safety Executive)

Local community (e.g. neighbours, former employees)

Fire and emergency services

Other organisations (e.g. British Coal, Opencast Executive, water, gas and power companies)

Technical literature (see industrial profiles in preparation by the Building Research Establishment for the Department of the Environment)

Sources of information on hydrological regime

British Geological Survey

National Rivers Authority

Water companies

Meteorological Office

Admiralty charts and tide tables (available from HMSO)

Source: reference 2

Appendix B Investigation techniques

Summary information on available techniques

Technique	Comments
Surface sampling e.g. stockpiled material, surface soils (down to 0.5 m), vegetation etc.	Inexpensive and easy to apply Gives early indication of immediate hazards No access to sub-surface conditions
Augers e.g. near surface soils	Relatively easy and inexpensive to apply in soft ground Gives preliminary impression of below ground conditions Samples may be cross-contaminated unless collected with care
Driven probes e.g. for soil, gas and liquid sampling	Cause minimal disturbance to ground Can accommodate a variety of monitoring devices once formed Ease of penetration depends on technique used May not provide good access for visual inspection of sub-surface conditions; however, some systems permit continuous encased soil sampling Most sophisticated techniques expensive to mobilise Provide advantages at exploratory investigation stage Provide advantage when investigating land contaminated with volatile compounds
Trial pits and trenches	Easy to apply and inexpensive Good access for inspection and sampling Depth limitation circa 6 m Site disturbance and potential for waste generation Exposes contamination to wind and water action
Boreholes	Permit sampling at depth Provide access for permanent sampling installations Less potential for waste generation Minimal above ground disturbance (but sub-surface impacts possible) May be suitable for integrated sampling (e.g. contamination-geological-hydrological) More expensive to install Restricted visual access to sub-surface conditions Drilling methods may impact on contaminant distributions

Summary information on available techniques — continued

Technique	Comments
Gas and groundwater monitoring wells	Can be installed to specific depths Can be used to monitor changes over time Minimal disturbance to ground Care needed during drilling and construction of monitoring installation Potential for migration of contaminants if poor design, construction or operation More expensive to install May be vulnerable to unauthorised disturbance unless properly protected

Source: reference 2

Appendix C Summary of capabilities and limitations of civil engineering based remedial methods

Excavation

Description

Excavation is the removal of contaminated solids and semi-solids from the site prior to disposal (off or on site) or treatment (on or off site) in a process-based system. Conventional civil engineering plant and equipment are used. The method is potentially widely applicable although the excavation of some materials (e.g. combustible, volatile, explosive or radioactive substances) should only proceed with extreme care and with suitable containment measures in place.

Potential advantages

— 'Permanent' solution for the site undergoing remediation provided all unacceptable material is removed
— Wide applicability
— Good potential for integration with other remedial methods
— Can deliver (uncontaminated) material for replacement purposes
— Proven technical capability
— Use of conventional, readily available plant
— Familiar to designers and contractors

Potential disadvantages

— When coupled with disposal does not reduce the volume or hazardous properties of contaminated material since it is only transferred elsewhere
— May be limitations on depth or extent of excavation (e.g. due to presence of services and buildings, effective reach of equipment, stability of ground)
— Excavation may need physical support
— May be a need to control surface/ground water regime
— Potential public health and environmental impacts from associated dust, gases, odours, vehicle and plant movements etc.
— Need for good characterisation of arisings to determine disposal/treatment routes
— Lack of suitable local disposal capacity (for off-site applications)
— Space, regulatory, engineering and post-treatment management implications associated with on-site disposal applications (see physical containment options)
— Regulatory controls on movement of hazardous wastes

Main requirements

— Good definition of boundaries of contamination
— Early identification of disposal/treatment route for arisings and methods of validating composition
— Early consultation with regulatory authorities if on-site disposal practised
— Strict controls over storage/segregation arrangements, particularly if site-won material is to be reused

Surface covers

Description   Surface covers are barriers placed over contaminated ground, primarily to isolate potential targets from underlying hazards. They may also be required to perform a wide range of other functions including restricting ingress of surface water, controlling upward migration of liquids and gases, providing a substrate for construction (including site services) or vegetation, and controlling odours, flies and vermin. Note that design objectives may conflict and this must be addressed at an early stage, usually by providing a multi-layered barrier. Cover systems alone may not be sufficient to reduce or control all the risks associated with the site (e.g. where soluble contaminants move laterally in groundwater, or gases migrate off-site through permeable strata).

Potential advantages
— May provide an economic solution on a large site provided that all potential hazards are addressed
— May improve the engineering properties of the site
— Use readily available material and conventional construction techniques and equipment
— Can be used in an interim or emergency capacity to meet an immediate need

Potential disadvantages
— Do not reduce the volume or hazardous properties of contaminants
— Integrity can be breached (e.g. by inadvertent human disturbance, tree roots, flooding etc.)
— Potential deterioration over the long term if adverse reactions occur between cover materials and contaminants
— Data on long-term performance sparse
— May restrict the future use of the site

Main requirements
— Design objectives must be explicit
— Specialist design and specification
— Placement of cover materials critical
— Early identification and thorough characterisation of cover materials
— Regular inspection and monitoring to demonstrate long-term performance
— Careful integration with in-ground barriers where appropriate
— Development of special protocols for maintenance/reinstatement

In-ground barriers

Description   In-ground barriers are physical structures used to prevent or restrict the lateral or vertical migration of contaminants (including gases) and movement of water into or out of a contaminated zone. Both vertical and horizontal barriers are available, although practical experience in the use of in-ground horizontal barriers for pollution control purposes is limited (apart from new landfill cells).

Vertical barriers can be classified according to the method of placement and include displacement (e.g. sheet steel piles), excavated (e.g. clay barriers, slurry trench) and injected (e.g. jet grouting) types. They are established techniques in conventional civil engineering terms and are finding increased application for pollution control purposes, particularly in relation to landfill.

Horizontal barriers may be used in conjunction with vertical barriers and surface covers to achieve complete encapsulation of a contaminant source (although in the UK a naturally occurring stratum of low permeability will often perform the same function). Emplacement typically relies on grouting techniques including jet, chemical and claquage grouting.

Potential advantages	— May offer an economic solution to large sites with significant migration potential — Applicable to a wide range of contaminants and media types — Use readily available and established techniques, equipment and materials — Minimal short-term environmental or public health impacts
Potential disadvantages	— Do not reduce the volume or hazardous properties of contaminated material — Are vulnerable to inadvertent disturbance (e.g. construction, maintenance work) — May deteriorate over time where adverse reaction occurs between contaminants and barrier materials — Installation may be difficult in variable ground or where obstructions are present — Lack of data on long-term performance — Need for long-term monitoring — May constrain future use of the site — May need to control hydrological regime
Main requirements	— Detailed contaminant/site characterisation, including geological and hydrological properties — Experienced design and construction — Long-term monitoring and maintenance — Depending on site-specific factors, may require waste management licence if used as part of an engineered on-site encapsulation facility

Hydraulic measures

Description

Hydraulic measures may be required to control the movement of surface or groundwater (e.g. during excavation), as an integral part of a remedial strategy (e.g. to maintain groundwater levels at required levels within and external to a barrier system, to increase the volume of unsaturated ground available to a soil vapour extraction system) or as the principal means of remediating the site (e.g. as part of a groundwater pump-to-treat operation). Hydraulic measures can also be used to contain and control a plume of contaminated groundwater to prevent it reaching a sensitive target (e.g. a drinking water abstraction well) or as an interim measure pending the implementation of more permanent measures.

Hydraulic controls rely on the use of established drainage and well pumping techniques and procedures. Specialist requirements arise because of contaminant behaviour in the water environment (e.g. they may be present as a floating phase, dissolved or dispersed in groundwater, or as a dense non-aqueous phase lying at the base of a contained aquifer) and because any contaminated liquids generated require special handling, treatment and disposal.

Potential advantages
— Provide a means of dealing with the contaminated aqueous environment
— Integration with other remedial methods relatively straightforward

— Systems are relatively flexible (e.g. additional wells can be installed or wells relocated) to cater for dynamic changes in sub-surface conditions
— Use familiar techniques and procedures

Potential disadvantages
— Duration and long-term performance of pump-to-treat operations may be uncertain
— Need to collect/treat/dispose of collected contaminated liquids
— Effectiveness of pumping operations may be limited by permeability characteristics of the ground
— Pumping operations may have adverse impacts on nearby buildings and services
— Ceasing to pump may result in a rise in concentration of contaminants in water

Main requirements
— Early consultation with regulatory authorities regarding abstraction/infiltration requirements
— Comprehensive characterisation of contaminants and site, including geological and hydrological properties
— Specialist input into design, construction, operation and maintenance of pumping systems, especially where used as the sole means of remediation
— On-going monitoring and adjustment in response to changes in sub-surface conditions

Appendix D Summary of capabilities and limitations of process-based remedial methods

Thermal processes

Description

Thermal processes involve the use of heat to remove, destroy or immobilise contaminants. Three main types of process are available:

— **thermal desorption** where volatile organic contaminants are removed from the host material and collected/treated (e.g. by incineration) in a second stage
— **incineration** where organic contaminants are oxidised at high temperature (some inorganic contaminants such as cyanide may be destroyed by thermal decomposition, metals may be present in the off-gases)
— **vitrification** where very high temperatures (up to 2000°C for some in-situ systems) are applied to destroy organic contaminants, trapping others (e.g. metals, asbestos) in a glassy product (metals may be present in the off-gases).

Thermal treatment processes may be applied in an ex- or in-situ mode. In-situ variants include hot air/steam stripping (where hot gases are introduced directly into the ground to strip volatile and semi-volatile contaminants from the unsaturated zone) and in-situ vitrification (where electrical energy is delivered through an array of electrodes inserted into the ground).

System configuration, processing parameters, operational requirements etc. are highly process- and site-specific. Mobile thermal desorption systems are in commercial use in the US; centralised/merchant incineration facilities, mainly for the treatment of hazardous waste, are available in the UK.

Potential advantages

— Can reduce hazardous properties of contaminated material
— Can provide a 'permanent' solution to the site being treated provided contaminants are completely removed/destroyed/immobilised

Potential disadvantages

— Energy intensive processes
— Effectiveness may vary depending on the chemical composition and physical characteristics of the feedstocks (ex-situ applications) or ground (in-situ applications) and on process conditions
— Some constituents of feedstock may cause fouling, blockages in the system
— Produce waste streams (e.g. gas and particulate emissions) that must be contained/treated to minimise public health and environmental impacts

— Health and safety implications associated with high temperatures and handling of potentially flammable/explosive gases
— Depending on applied temperatures, treated material may undergo physical/chemical/biological changes that may reduce its value for construction/landscape purposes

Main requirements
— Good characterisation of contaminants and host material (or ground conditions in in-situ applications)
— May require pre-treatment (e.g. size reduction/screening, drying) of feedstocks in ex-situ applications
— Careful control over process conditions (e.g. temperature, residence times, mixing)
— Efficient emission control equipment
— Ambient air quality monitoring may be required to demonstrate compliance with agreed limits

Physical processes

Description

These methods rely on physical processes to separate contaminants from the host medium, or, in ex-situ systems, to separate out different fractions of material having different contaminant characteristics.

A wide range of methods are potentially available although only a few systems are in commercial use for the treatment of contaminated land. These include:

— **soils washing** (ex-situ and in-situ variations available) in which an aqueous washing medium is used to remove (by mechanical scrubbing action) contaminants from soil particle surfaces and to separate out coarse (generally uncontaminated) and fine (generally contaminated) soil fractions
— **solvent extraction** (ex-situ) in which a non-aqueous solvent (e.g. triethylamine, liquified propane) is used to remove contaminants preferentially from the host material
— **electrokinetics** (in-situ) where an electric field is applied to force the migration of contaminants through the soil to collection points where they are recovered/treated
— **soil vapour extraction** (in-situ) in which volatile contaminants are stripped from the unsaturated zone in a reduced pressure air flow.

System configuration, processing parameters, operational requirements etc. are highly process- and site-specific. Ex-situ soils washing systems and soil vapour extraction are in commercial use in Europe and are available in the UK. Solvent extraction and in-situ electro-reclamation have been demonstrated at a field scale in the US and the Netherlands respectively.

Potential advantages
— Can reduce the volume of hazardous material
— Can provide a 'permanent' solution to the site being treated provided that all the contaminants are removed

Potential disadvantages
— Produce waste streams that must be treated/disposed of
— Effectiveness may vary depending on feedstock type/ground conditions and operational parameters
— May be public health/environmental impacts through process emissions (e.g. volatile organic compounds in soil vapour extraction systems)

— May be occupational health and safety implications associated with treatment agents (e.g. solvents, chemicals used to treat spent washing solutions)
— May be difficult to demonstrate end-point for in-situ systems

Main requirements
— Good characterisation of contaminants, feedstocks/ground conditions
— Intimate mixing between contaminants/treatment agent (this may be limited in in-situ applications where soils have low gas/liquid permeabilities)
— Pre-treatment (e.g. size reduction, screening) of feedstocks may be required in ex-situ applications
— Careful control over process conditions (e.g. formulation of treatment agent, contact times, mixing)
— Some systems have good potential for integration with other remedial techniques (e.g. treatment of organically loaded fine solids fraction of soils washing plant via incineration, biological treatment; use of electrokinetic techniques as a means of introducing treatment agents into the ground)

Chemical processes

Description

These methods rely on chemical reactions to destroy or change the hazardous properties of contaminants. Conceptually, a wide variety of chemical agents and reactions could be used to deal with the contaminants present on the site. In practice, few chemical treatment processes are feasible (or commercially available) because site conditions (types, concentrations and distribution of contaminants, composition of the host media) are often too heterogenous to predict the outcome of chemical treatment reliably. Methods that have been demonstrated in the field include:

— dechlorination, for example using a potassium hydroxide/polyethylene glygolate reagent to treat soils contaminated with polychlorinated biphenyls (PCBs)
— in-situ soil leaching using chemically modified (addition of acids, bases, surfactants etc.) leach solutions to remove contaminants.

Two dechlorination methods (KPEG, BCD) have been demonstrated at field-scale in the US. Acidified leach solutions have been used to remove cadmium from soils in the Netherlands.

Potential advantages
— Can reduce the hazardous properties of contaminated materials
— Can provide a 'permanent' solution for the site undergoing treatment provided that all contaminants are removed/destroyed/modified

Potential disadvantages
— Produce waste streams that may require further treatment/disposal
— Difficulty in formulating appropriate treatment agent where mixtures of contaminants are present
— Outcome of chemical reaction may be difficult to predict where site conditions are complex
— Treatment agents themselves may pose health or environmental hazards
— Further treatment may be required to remove excess reagents, by-products and wastes from treated material

Main requirements
— Good characterisation of contaminants, feedstocks/ground conditions
— Intimate mixing between contaminants/treatment agent (this may be limited in in-situ applications where soils have low gas/liquid permeabilities)

— Pre-treatment (e.g. size reduction, screening, dewatering) of feedstocks may be required in ex-situ applications
— Requires careful control over process conditions (e.g. formulation of treatment agent, contact times, mixing).
— May be difficult to demonstrate end-point in in-situ applications

Biological processes

Description

Biological processes use the natural metabolic pathways of living organisms (typically microbial agents, but also higher plants) to destroy, remove or transform contaminants into a less hazardous form. Both indigenous and laboratory cultured biological agents may be used.

All biological treatment methods aim to optimise the level of biological activity by providing a suitable food substrate (this may be the target contaminant or an organic amendment), other essential nutrients, appropriate oxygen levels (both aerobic and anaerobic systems are possible), pH, temperature etc. Two main approaches are in commercial use for the treatment of contaminated sites:

— ex-situ treatment in engineered beds or bioreactors
— in-situ treatment in which biodegradation processes are enhanced by the direct addition of oxygen, nutrients etc. into the ground.

Bioreactors (dry or slurry types for solids, trickling filter and activated sludge types for liquids) allow greater control over process conditions than engineered beds, and treatment duration may be reduced as a result. Covering or the addition of heat can enhance treatment rates in engineered systems.

Potential advantages

— Can reduce the hazardous properties of contaminated material
— Can provide a 'permanent' solution to the site being remediated provided that contaminants are destroyed or transformed to innocuous substances

Potential disadvantages

— Can produce substances that are more toxic/mobile than the target compound
— Some organic compounds are not easily degraded even under optimum conditions
— Substances (e.g. metals, pesticides) may be present that inhibit biological activity
— May be a need to contain gas emissions/odours produced during processing

Main requirements

— Good characterisation of feedstocks/ground conditions
— May need provision of nutrients etc.
— On-going monitoring/adjustment to maintain optimum growth conditions
— Effective contact/mixing between biological agents and contaminants
— Flow-through systems require physical support structures to maintain optimal biological mass
— May need to smooth out fluctuations in contaminant concentrations to avoid toxic shock effects at front end of flow-through systems
— May need to collect/contain leachates produced in engineered beds, and gases/odours produced during treatment in enclosed reactors
— May be difficult to demonstrate end-point in in-situ applications

Stabilisation/ solidification processes

Description

These methods involve the chemical stabilisation/immobilisation of contaminants within a solid matrix that has favourable leaching characteristics. Both ex-situ and in-situ variants are available. A range of binding materials are commercially available: many have proprietary status. Common formulations include those based on cement, silicates, lime, thermoplastics and polymers.

Cement-based systems have been used extensively and are considered 'proven' in the US for the treatment of inorganic contaminants, such as metals. They are considered less effective for the treatment of organic contaminants and both organic, and some inorganic, species may interfere with binding and setting processes. Systems based on organophilic clays are under development for the treatment of organic and mixed materials.

Long-term performance data for stabilised/solidified material are generally lacking.

Potential advantages

— Use conventional equipment and readily available materials
— Reduce the hazardous properties of contaminated materials, at least over the short term
— May improve the handling or engineering properties of treated material
— Integration with other forms of treatment relatively straightforward (e.g. treatment of incineration products to improve leaching characteristics)

Potential disadvantages

— Difficulty in selecting suitable reagent when complex mixture of contaminants is present
— Long-term performance uncertain
— May increase the volume of material to be handled on the site
— Implications for construction/installation of services if treated material replaced on the site
— Monitoring of treated material may be required to demonstrate effectiveness over the long term
— Potential for health and environmental impact (e.g. exothermic reaction of some processes may release volatile constituents from feedstocks, dusts may be released during handling/storage of reagents)

Main requirements

— Good characterisation of contaminants, feedstocks/ground conditions
— Intimate mixing between contaminants/treatment agent
— Pre-treatment (e.g. size reduction, screening) of feedstocks may be required in ex-situ applications
— Requires careful control over process conditions (e.g. formulation of treatment agent, contact times, mixing)
— May be difficult to demonstrate end-point in in-situ applications

Appendix E Initial selection criteria

Initial selection criteria for remedial works

Criterion	Implications for selection
Applicability	Relates to contaminants and media (soils, sediments, liquid effluents etc.) to be treated; note that some process-based methods are applicable only to a narrow range of contaminants (e.g. soil vapour extraction to volatile organic substances)
Effectiveness	Ability to achieve specified CROs; note that effectiveness should be measured in terms of residual concentrations remaining after treatment — methods having a high removal or destruction efficiency may still leave unacceptable concentrations if initial levels are high
Limitations	Limitations may be inherent (e.g. inability to destroy most inorganic contaminants thermally) or site-specific (e.g. limitation on excavation close to built services or structures, inability to locate large items of process plant on a small site)
Cost	Costs can vary significantly depending on the proposed remedial method and site characteristics; comparisons under the same cost heads can assist in initial selection; capital, operational and on-going (e.g. post-treatment monitoring) costs should all be addressed
Development status	The development status of a remedial method clearly has implications for the commercial and technical risks associated with the remedial project; innovative methods are also likely to be more demanding in terms of bench or pilot-scale testing
Availability	Availability of the required plant, equipment and personnel affects the feasibility of employing a remedial method in practice, particularly if the source (of equipment, expertise etc.) is primarily located overseas
Operational requirements	Use of a method may be restricted by a lack of operational support including, for example: legal approval; site services; working space; access; laboratory support; handling/disposal of residues etc.

Initial selection criteria for remedial works — continued

Criterion	Implications for selection
Information requirements	Remedial methods have specific information requirements which must be satisfied before a final decision is made on their suitability for use. Examples include: volatility of contaminants, permeability characteristics of site (for soil vapour extraction); particle size characteristics, partitioning behaviour, presence of potential reactive substances etc. (for soils washing methods); degradability characteristics, presence of inhibitory compounds etc. (for biological treatment methods)
Planning and management needs	Important for all methods but may be limiting for some, depending on the circumstances of the site (e.g. lack of time to obtain necessary legal approvals, lack of time/expertise to develop necessary technical specifications etc.)
Health and safety aspects	Important for all methods but may be more demanding for some: in general, in-situ applications reduce health and safety implications but may increase risk of below ground environmental impacts (see below)
Potential for integration	Important where an integrated remedial system is being proposed; will have implications for programming of work activities, access and storage arrangements, provision of site services etc.
Environmental impacts	Vary depending on the method being considered and site characteristics; will have implications for control measures and the extent and type of monitoring undertaken
Monitoring requirements	Vary depending on the method being considered, extent of regulatory involvement and site characteristics: some remedial methods (e.g. containment) may have very demanding monitoring implications (see below)
Validation requirements	Vary depending on methods being considered (e.g. sampling and testing of excavated area before replacement with clean, inert fill; sampling and testing of product from a thermal, biological or physical treatment plant)
Post-treatment management requirements	Vary depending on the methods being considered and may be considerable where contaminants are to be retained on site (e.g. beneath a covering system, within an encapsulation cell, in a stabilised/solidified form) or where the end-point of remedial action is difficult to determine (e.g. in a pump-and-treat operation, in-situ biological or chemical treatment); may involve both technical (e.g. groundwater quality monitoring) and administrative requirements (e.g. restrictions on the use of certain areas of the site, permitted construction methods)

References

1. SMITH M. A. (ed.) *Contaminated land: reclamation and treatment.* Report of the NATO Committee on Challenges to Modern Society Pilot Study on Contaminated Land. Plenum Press, London, 1985.
2. HARRIS M. R., HERBERT S. M. and SMITH M. A. *CIRIA SP 101-112: The remedial treatment of contaminated land.* CIRIA, London, (1994, in press).
3. STEEDS J. E., SHEPHERD E. and BARRY D. L. *A guide to safe working practices for contaminated sites.* CIRIA, London, (1994, in press).
4. DENNER J. *Industrial Waste Management.* Update on UK Policy, September 1993, 8–9.
5. PETTS J. Dealing with contaminated land within a risk management framework. *Proceedings of the 5th Annual Conference on Contaminated Land: Policy, Risk Management and Technology.* Paper No. 2. IBC Technical Services, London, 1994.
6. ROYAL SOCIETY. *Risk: analysis, perception and management.* Royal Society, London, 1992.
7. INTERDEPARTMENTAL COMMITTEE ON THE REDEVELOPMENT OF CONTAMINATED LAND. *Guidance on the assessment and redevelopment of contaminated land: ICRCL 59/83.* ICRCL, 2nd edn, 1987 (available from the Department of the Environment Publications Sales Unit, Eastcote).
8. DEPARTMENT OF THE ENVIRONMENT. *Landfill gas.* Waste Management Paper No. 27, 2nd edn, HMSO, London, 1991.
9. SITE INVESTIGATION STEERING GROUP. Without site investigation ground is a hazard. *Site investigation in construction.* Vol. 1, Thomas Telford, London, 1993.
10. SITE INVESTIGATION STEERING GROUP. Guidelines for the safe investigation by drilling of landfills and contaminated land. *Site investigation in construction.* Vol. 4, Thomas Telford, London, 1993.
11. BRITISH STANDARDS INSTITUTION. *Draft for development code of practice on the identification of potentially contaminated land and its investigation, BS DD 175.* BSI, London, 1988.
12. BRITISH STANDARDS INSTITUTION. *Code of practice for site investigations, BS 5930.* BSI, London, 1981. (Note: this Standard is currently being updated, 1994).
13. SCOTTISH ENTERPRISE. *Requirements for contaminated land site investigations, Revision 0,T.* SE Environmental Department, Glasgow, January, 1993.
14. UNITED STATES ENVIRONMENTAL PROTECTION AGENCY. *Handbook of suggested practices for the design and installation of groundwater monitoring wells.* EPA/600/4-89/034, USEPA, Washington DC, 1991.
15. STANDING COMMITTEE OF ANALYSTS. *Methods for the examination of waters and associated materials.* (Various titles), HMSO, London, (various dates).
16. FERGUSON C. A statistical basis for spatial sampling of contaminated land. *Ground Engineering,* 1992, **25**, No. 5, 34–38.

17. HEALTH AND SAFETY EXECUTIVE. *Protection of workers and the general public during the development of contaminated land, HS(G) 66.* HMSO, London, 1991.

18. BRITISH STANDARDS INSTITUTION. *Quality Systems, BS 5750.* BSI, London, 1987.

19. ANON. *Soil clean-up guidelines (Leidraad bodemsaniering).* Dutch Ministry of Housing, Physical Planning and the Environment, The Hague (SDU), 1987. (Note: revisions expected 1994.)

20. CANADIAN COUNCIL OF MINISTERS OF THE ENVIRONMENT. *Interim Canadian environmental quality criteria for contaminated sites, CCME EPC-CS34.* CCME, Winnipeg, September 1991.

21. AUSTRALIAN AND NEW ZEALAND ENVIRONMENT AND CONSERVATION COUNCIL/NATIONAL HEALTH AND MEDICAL RESEARCH COUNCIL. *Australian and New Zealand guidelines for the assessment and management of contaminated sites,* ANZECC/HHMRC, 1992.

22. BUILDING RESEARCH ESTABLISHMENT. *Construction of new buildings on gas-contaminated land.* BRE, Watford, 1991.

23. INTERDEPARTMENTAL COMMITTEE ON THE REDEVELOPMENT OF CONTAMINATED LAND. *Notes on the development and afteruse of landfill sites: ICRCL 17/78.* ICRCL, 8th edn, 1990 (available from Department of the Environment Publications Sales Unit, Eastcote).

24. CARD G. B. *Protecting development from methane.* CIRIA Core Programme Funders Report CP/8 CIRIA, London, 1994.

25. HARRIES C. R., WITHERINGTON P. J. and McENTEE J. M. *Interpreting measurements of gas in the ground.* CIRIA Core Programme Funders Report CP/22. CIRIA, London, 1994.

26. O'RIORDAN N. J. and MILLOY C. J. *Risk assessment for methane and other gases from the ground.* CIRIA Core Programme Funders Report CP/23. CIRIA, London, 1994.

27. INSTITUTE OF PETROLEUM. *Code of practice for the investigation and mitigation of possible petroleum-based land contamination.* IP/Wiley, London, 1993.

28. MINISTRY OF AGRICULTURE, FISHERIES AND FOOD/WELSH OFFICE AGRICULTURE DEPARTMENT. *Code of good agricultural practice for the protection of soil.* Consultation paper, MAFF, London, 1992.

29. HARRIS R. Contaminated land and water quality standards. *Proceedings of the 5th Annual Conference on Contaminated Land: Policy, Risk Management and Technology.* Paper No. 9. IBC Technical Services, London, 1994.

30. ANON. *Pollution Handbook.* National Society for Clean Air and Environmental Protection, London, 1992.

31. HEALTH AND SAFETY EXECUTIVE. *Occupational exposure limits, EH 40.* HMSO, London, 1993.

32. DEPARTMENT OF THE ENVIRONMENT. *Problems arising from the redevelopment of gasworks and similar sites.* 2nd edn, HMSO, London, 1987.

33. UNITED STATES ENVIRONMENTAL PROTECTION AGENCY. *Risk assessment guidance for Superfund: human health evaluation manual.* Part A, EPA/540/1-89/002. USEPA Office of Emergency and Remedial Response, Washington, DC, 1989.

34. DEPARTMENT OF THE ENVIRONMENT. *Special wastes: a technical memorandum providing guidance on their definition.* Waste Management Paper No. 23. HMSO, London, 1981.

35. HEALTH AND SAFETY EXECUTIVE. *Risk criteria for land-use planning in the vicinity of major industrial hazards.* HMSO, London, 1989.

36. ARMISHAW R. *et al. Review of innovative soil clean-up processes.* Report LR 819 (MR). Warren Spring Laboratory, 1992.

37. UNITED STATES ENVIRONMENTAL PROTECTION AGENCY. *Innovative treatment technologies: overview and guide to information sources*. EPA/540/9-91/002. USEPA Office of Solid Waste and Emergency Response, Washington, DC, 1991.

38. UNITED STATES ENVIRONMENTAL PROTECTION AGENCY. *The Superfund Innovative Technology Evaluation Program: Technology Profiles*. EPA/540/R-92/077. 5th edn, USEPA Office of Solid Waste and Emergency Response, Washington, DC, 1992.

39. UNITED STATES ENVIRONMENTAL PROTECTION AGENCY. *Guide for conducting treatability studies under CERCLA. Final report, EPA/540/R-92/07a*. USEPA Office of Solid Waste and Emergency Response, Washington, DC, 1992.

40. BARBER J. N. *Quality management in construction — contractual aspects*. Special Publication 84, CIRIA, London, 1992.

41. OLIVER G. B. M. *Quality management in construction: interpretations of BS 5750 (1987) — 'Quality Management Systems' for the construction industry*. Special Publication 74, CIRIA, London, 1990.

42. ANON. *A client's guide to design-and-build*. Special Publication 15. CIRIA, London, 1981.

43. INSTITUTION OF CIVIL ENGINEERS, ASSOCIATION OF CONSULTING ENGINEERS AND FEDERATION OF CIVIL ENGINEERING CONTRACTORS. *ICE Conditions of contract and forms of tender, agreement and bond for use in connection with works of civil engineering construction*. 6th edn, Thomas Telford, London, 1991.

44. INSTITUTION OF CIVIL ENGINEERS. *Civil engineering standard method of measurement*. 3rd edn, Thomas Telford, London, 1991.

45. INSTITUTION OF CIVIL ENGINEERS, ASSOCIATION OF CONSULTING ENGINEERS AND FEDERATION OF CIVIL ENGINEERING CONTRACTORS. *ICE Design and construct conditions of contract*. Thomas Telford, London, 1992.

46. INSTITUTION OF CHEMICAL ENGINEERS. *Model forms of conditions of contract for process plant*. Institution of Chemical Engineers, 1992.